The body of an American soldier killed during
the Battle of the Bulge is carried in from a snowy
Ardennes field by German prisoners. The
six-week battle—the biggest in Western Europe
during the Second World War—claimed more
than 160,000 American and German casualties.

THE BATTLE OF THE BULGE

WORLD WAR II · TIME-LIFE BOOKS · ALEXANDRIA, VIRGINIA

BY WILLIAM K. GOOLRICK AND OGDEN TANNER

AND THE EDITORS OF TIME-LIFE BOOKS

THE BATTLE OF THE BULGE

Time-Life Books Inc.
is a wholly owned subsidiary of
TIME INCORPORATED

Founder: Henry R. Luce 1898-1967

Editor-in-Chief: Henry Anatole Grunwald
Chairman of the Board: Andrew Heiskell
President: James R. Shepley
Editorial Director: Ralph Graves
Vice Chairman: Arthur Temple

TIME-LIFE BOOKS INC.

Managing Editor: Jerry Korn
Executive Editor: David Maness
Assistant Managing Editors: Dale M. Brown
(planning), George Constable, George G. Daniels
(acting), Martin Mann, John Paul Porter
Art Director: Tom Suzuki
Chief of Research: David L. Harrison
Director of Photography: Robert G. Mason
Senior Text Editor: Diana Hirsh
Assistant Art Director: Arnold C. Holeywell
Assistant Chief of Research: Carolyn L. Sackett
Assistant Director of Photography: Dolores A. Littles

Chairman: Joan D. Manley
President: John D. McSweeney
Executive Vice Presidents: Carl G. Jaeger,
John Steven Maxwell, David J. Walsh
Vice Presidents: Nicholas Benton (public
relations), John L. Canova (sales),
Nicholas J. C. Ingleton (Asia), James L. Mercer
(Europe/South Pacific), Herbert Sorkin
(production), Paul R. Stewart (promotion),
Peter G. Barnes
Personnel Director: Beatrice T. Dobie
Consumer Affairs Director: Carol Flaumenhaft
Comptroller: George Artandi

WORLD WAR II

Editorial Staff for *The Battle of the Bulge*
Editor: Gerald Simons
Picture Editor/Designer: Raymond Ripper
Text Editors: Brian McGinn, Lydia Preston,
Henry Woodhead
Staff Writers: Susan Bryan, Dalton Delan,
Kumait Jawdat, Tyler Mathisen, John Newton,
Teresa M. C. R. Pruden
Chief Researcher: Oobie Gleysteen
Researchers: Kristin Baker, Marion F. Briggs,
Mary G. Burns, Jane Edwin, Judy Shanks,
Jean Strong
Art Assistant: Mary Louise Mooney
Editorial Assistant: Connie Strawbridge

Editorial Production
Production Editor: Douglas B. Graham
Operations Manager: Gennaro C. Esposito,
Gordon E. Buck (assistant)
Assistant Production Editor: Feliciano Madrid
Quality Control: Robert L. Young (director),
James J. Cox (assistant), Michael G. Wight
(associate)
Art Coordinator: Anne B. Landry
Copy Staff: Susan B. Galloway (chief),
Eleanore W. Karsten, Peter Kaufman, Victoria Lee,
Celia Beattie
Picture Department: Alvin L. Ferrell
Traffic: Jeanne Potter

Correspondents: Elisabeth Kraemer (Bonn);
Margot Hapgood, Dorothy Bacon, Lesley Coleman
(London); Susan Jonas, Lucy T. Voulgaris (New
York); Maria Vincenza Aloisi, Josephine du Brusle
(Paris); Ann Natanson (Rome). Valuable assistance
was also provided by Wibo van de Linde
(Amsterdam); Brigid Grauman, Chris Redman
(Brussels); Anne Angus, Karin Pearce, Pat Stimpson
(London); Carolyn T. Chubet, Miriam Hsia (New
York); Mary Martin (Ottawa); Traudl Lessing
(Vienna); Bogdan Turek (Warsaw).

The Co-authors: WILLIAM K. GOOLRICK served
on General George S. Patton Jr.'s staff in North
Africa, Sicily, England and France. During the Battle of the Bulge he was with the headquarters of
the 80th Division. A graduate of the Virginia Military Institute, he earned his M.A. in English lit-
erature at Columbia University. He worked on
LIFE for a decade, and later became a senior editor of the *Saturday Evening Post.* He is a former
editor of TIME-LIFE BOOKS' Human Behavior and
World War II series.

OGDEN TANNER, a freelance writer and editor
with wide-ranging interests, has been a feature
writer for the San Francisco *Chronicle,* assistant
managing editor of *Architectural Forum* and a senior editor of TIME-LIFE BOOKS. He is the author of
several other volumes for TIME-LIFE BOOKS,
among them *New England Wilds* and *Urban Wilds*
in the American Wilderness series; *The Canadians*
and *The Ranchers* in the Old West series; *Stress* in
the Human Behavior series, and three volumes in
The TIME-LIFE Encyclopedia of Gardening. During
World War II he served in the U.S. Navy.

The Consultants: COLONEL JOHN R. ELTING, USA
(Ret.), is a military historian and author of *The
Battle of Bunker's Hill, The Battles of Saratoga* and
Military History and Atlas of the Napoleonic Wars.
He edited *Military Uniforms in America: The Era
of the American Revolution, 1755-1795* and *Mili-
tary Uniforms of America: Years of Growth, 1796-
1851,* and was associate editor of *The West Point
Atlas of American Wars.*

CHARLES B. MACDONALD fought as a rifle company commander in the Battle of the Bulge and
recounted his experiences in *Company Commander.* He supervised preparation of the official
U.S. Army history of the war in Europe, writing
two of the volumes, *The Siegfried Line Campaign*
and *The Last Offensive,* and is currently the Depu-
ty Chief Historian for Southeast Asia in the U.S.
Army Center of Military History. His other books
include *The Battle of the Huertgen Forest* and *The
Mighty Endeavor: American Armed Forces in the
European Theater in World War II.*

Library of Congress Cataloging in Publication Data

Goolrick, William K 1920-
    The Battle of the Bulge.

    (World War II; v. 18)
    Bibliography: p.
    Includes index.
    1. Ardennes, Battle of the, 1944-1945. I. Tanner, Ogden,
joint author. II. Time-Life Books. III. Title. IV. Series.
D756.5.A7G66   940.54'21   79-5184
ISBN 0-8094-2532-7
ISBN 0-8094-2531-9 lib. bdg.

CHAPTERS

1: Hitler's Master Stroke   20

2: A Wave of Terror   48

3: The Big Breakthrough   82

4: Battle for Saint-Vith   110

5: The Siege of Bastogne   148

6: The German High Tide   178

PICTURE ESSAYS

The War's Wettest Campaign   6

Happy Days in the Ardennes   36

The German Juggernaut   66

The All-Purpose Engineers   96

The GI vs. Winter   122

A Wounded GI's Odyssey   134

Tankers to the Rescue   164

The Civilians' Plight   190

Acknowledgments   204
Bibliography   204
Picture Credits   205
Index   206

CONTENTS

LCA 1134

THE WAR'S WETTEST CAMPAIGN

Supply-laden British landing craft are unloaded on a mucky beach near Flushing, Holland, during the Allies' struggle to clear Germans from the Schelde Estuary.

A TWO-PRONGED ATTACK TO OPEN A VITAL PORT

In October 1944, two months before the German counter-offensive that touched off the Battle of the Bulge, the course of that enormous struggle was strongly influenced by bitter fighting along Holland's Schelde Estuary.

The victorious Allied armies, racing north and east toward Germany from their invasion beachhead in Normandy, had stretched their supply lines to the breaking point. Tanks were out of gas, rations were in short supply, ammunition stocks were dangerously low. Each Allied division required an average of 500 tons of matériel every day, and only a fraction of that amount could be delivered by truck convoys from the port of Cherbourg, some 350 miles to the rear.

The Allies desperately needed a first-class port near the new front lines. In theory, they already had one in Antwerp, which had been occupied so swiftly by the British on September 4 that the retreating Germans had been unable to dynamite its 26 miles of docks. Unfortunately for the Allies, however, the use of this perfect port was denied them by German troops, who had mined the 60-mile-long Schelde Estuary between Antwerp and the North Sea, and who were defending the river's mouth with a formidable concentration of 67 big naval guns.

To rout the Germans from the Schelde, the men of the Canadian First Army attacked along both sides of the estuary—and soon found themselves mired in one of the nastiest campaigns of the War. The defenders had opened the dikes, which flooded the surrounding low-lying land, and had fortified the only high ground—man-made banks and causeways. Canadians of the II Corps, attacking the Germans in the Breskens pocket *(opposite)* on the south bank, all but drowned in what one war correspondent called "the grimmest piece of 'ground' over which men have ever been called upon to fight."

At the cost of 13,000 casualties, the Canadians cleared the Schelde and opened the waterway to Antwerp. Matériel from the port eventually solved the Allies' supply problem. But the gallant defenders had helped the Germans gain time to regroup for the Ardennes counteroffensive.

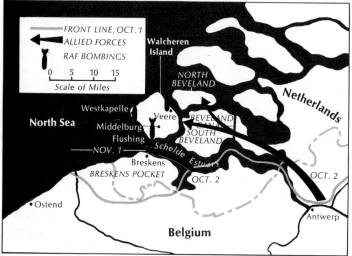

In early October, 1944, the Canadian First Army launched a double-barreled attack to clear the Germans from the Schelde Estuary. While one force eliminated the Germans' Breskens pocket south of the Schelde, a second force advanced north from Antwerp and then west across South Beveland to the last German stronghold on Walcheren Island, which had been bombed by the RAF as shown. In the final assault on Walcheren, two British forces made amphibious landings at Flushing and Westkapelle.

German soldiers, dug in atop a dike in the Breskens pocket south of the Schelde Estuary, man their guns and await the Canadians attacking from the east.

An RAF aerial photograph of Walcheren's southern coast shows torrents of sea water rushing inland through gaps bombed in the sea wall east of Flushing.

Farms west of Flushing lie under water that poured through the bomb-breached sea wall at upper right. In the distance stand tall cranes in Flushing's harbor.

Trundling through a flooded village street, a Dutch farming family sets out for higher ground in a horse-drawn cart loaded down with valuable possessions.

FLOODING THE GERMANS' ISLAND STRONGHOLD

As Canadian infantrymen began slogging through flooded fields on both sides of the Schelde, the Allies did some flooding of their own, inundating the formidable German defenses on Walcheren Island, the ultimate objective of the campaign. On October 2, leaflets dropped by American planes warned the island's inhabitants that flooding was imminent. The next day, 259 RAF bombers blasted a 75-yard gap in the immense dike on Walcheren's western tip. The bombers later returned to rupture the dikes near Flushing and Veere.

The island's low-lying interior was soon under several feet of water, and the Germans' inland gun positions were flooded. But as the assault forces would learn to their sorrow, neither bombs nor water did much damage to the Germans' big coastal guns, which were safely emplaced on the elevated sea wall.

A Dutchwoman in native costume hands her suitcase to men rescuing her from Walcheren's interior.

11

Canadian troops salvage a prime mover that skidded off a slippery road and into a flooded field.

THE FIGHTING ON THE NORTHERN SHORE

Slowly, painfully, the right wing of the Canadian First Army pushed its way north from Antwerp toward the isthmus leading to South Beveland, the peninsula forming the Schelde's northern shore. The men met such stiff German resistance that it took them two weeks to advance 15 miles to the neck of the isthmus. And to make matters worse, heavy rains turned the countryside into a nearly impassable quagmire.

The struggle along the isthmus' single narrow causeway proved to be a nightmare for the attackers, who were felled in droves by shellbursts from German mortars and the dreaded 88mm guns. And then forward units were stopped by the five-mile-long Beveland Canal, a heavily defended waterway that was as wide at some points as 290 feet.

On the night of October 27, soldiers of the Canadian 6th Infantry Brigade paddled across the canal in small boats and established bridgeheads in the ooze on the far side. On the following day, engineers threw a pontoon bridge over the canal, enabling the troops and tanks to continue westward across the widening peninsula. Finally, on October 31, they fought their way across a causeway and attacked the German defenders on Walcheren Island.

A double file of military vehicles (above) stretches along the causeway on the South Beveland isthmus, waiting for the canal up ahead to be bridged by engineers.

Later, tanks (above, right) rumble across the pontoon bridge. Beside it lies the useless main drawbridge, which was dynamited by the Germans as they retreated.

A PAIR OF BLOODY AMPHIBIOUS ASSAULTS

The battle for the Schelde climaxed on November 1 at dawn, when two forces of British Commandos hit the beaches on Walcheren. One force had come from Ostend aboard a fleet of landing craft supported by warships, including the old battleship *Warspite*, whose 15-inch guns were expected to help silence the big German shore batteries at the appointed beachhead on the western tip of the island.

The concrete gun emplacements, however, withstood the *Warspite*'s bombardment, and when four Commando units— some 1,000 men in all—streamed ashore near Westkapelle, they were blasted by cannon fire and mowed down by machine guns. Every soldier in the leading troop of No. 48 Commando was killed or wounded while storming one German battery. By the second evening, some 370 British were lying dead or wounded. Heavy losses were also suffered by the Royal Navy, whose men crewed landing craft and fire-support ships. Of the 27 close-support craft, only seven were fit for action after the assault.

But the Westkapelle assault force slowly widened its beachheads, and so did the second assault force, which had embarked from captured Breskens to Flushing, on the southern shore of Walcheren. On the 3rd of November, the two forces managed to link up and the Schelde Estuary was at last in Allied hands—along with 41,000 German prisoners of war.

Covered by a British naval bombardment, a big LCT

Battle-ready British Commandos aboard a landing craft cast off at Breskens, bound for Flushing.

(right) *and small amphibious vehicles chug toward Westkapelle. Many of the amphibians reached the beach but were set afire by enemy artillery and mines.*

A fire-support ship sinks off Westkapelle, its hull riddled by a shore battery. Such ships attracted German fire, thus helping the Commandos to reach shore.

Scots of the 52nd Lowland Division, following the Commandos into Flushing, take cover from German fire at the foot of an enormous dockside crane.

Men of the King's Own Scottish Borderers attack down a narrow, rubble-strewn street in Flushing. The Germans defended the town building by building.

Captured by British troops, German prisoners cluster on a patch of high ground in the town of Middelburg in the flooded interior of Walcheren Island.

The German commander on Walcheren, Lieut. General Wilhelm Daser, surrenders to the British in Middelburg.

A German mine exploded at water's edge by British engineers sends up a shower of water and concrete particles from the docking installation at left. The Germans sank the ship in the background to block access to the dock.

The first Allied cargo ship to enter the harbor at Antwerp, the Canadian-built Liberty ship Fort Cataraqui, steams past a pier on the 28th of November, 1944. By the end of the following month, supplies averaging 22,300 tons a day were being unloaded by the port's 600 cranes.

CLEARING MINES FOR A FLOW OF SUPPLIES

Immediately after the great guns on Walcheren Island had been knocked out, more than 100 Royal Navy minesweepers began clearing the Schelde Estuary. It was a long and perilous task.

Some of the mines, anchored to the bottom, were cut free by towed cables and then exploded by rifle fire as they bobbed to the surface. Other mines were designed to be detonated by the magnetic field of an approaching ship or by the noise of its propellers. So wooden or demagnetized minesweepers were used, fitted with special equipment that projected electric impulses and sound waves through the water to explode the mines at a safe distance.

This nerve-racking work went on for 22 days. Eventually, after the Royal Navy had blown up or disarmed 267 German mines, the Schelde was declared safe for shipping.

The opening of Antwerp's vast harbor came none too soon. The German defenders and their mines had prevented the Allies from using the port for 85 days after its capture, and just 18 days were left before the Germans launched their massive counteroffensive in the Ardennes.

1

Hitler plans "another Dunkirk" for the Allies
Raising new divisions for the imperiled Third Reich
The Führer's mysterious ailment
An ill-starred airborne assault
The Canadians' struggle to open a crucial port
Attacking Germany's formidable West Wall
The first German city falls to the Allies
The fight for a deadly forest
Artful deception hides three armies
"Give all for our Fatherland and our Führer!"
The Americans receive a last-minute warning

The plan that led to the War's biggest battle in Western Europe took shape gradually in the mind of Adolf Hitler. It was a plan born of desperation in July of 1944 and nurtured on bad news all through August. Day after day, grim reports from the far-flung battlefronts greeted Hitler at the Wolf's Lair, his secret headquarters deep in a forest near Rastenburg, East Prussia. Every day the battle maps showed that an iron ring of enemy armies was closing in on Germany from almost every direction.

On the Eastern front, the Russians had smashed 25 German divisions—the worst defeat that had ever been inflicted on the German Army—and were overrunning Poland on their way to the border of East Prussia.

In Italy, the Allies had captured Rome and were attacking the German line 155 miles farther north.

In France, American and British forces had burst out of their invasion beachhead in Normandy, virtually annihilating two German armies in the process. They were now driving northeast through Belgium and northern France toward the German border. A second invasion force of Americans and Free French racing from the Riviera up the Rhone Valley had entrapped a small part of a third German army. The shattered remnants of German units in the west were scrambling homeward in disarray.

In spite of the Wehrmacht's crushing defeats, Hitler believed that the tide of battle could be reversed. He reasoned that the Allied armies had come so far so fast that they would have to halt until their supplies caught up with them, and until their exhausted divisions had been rested, refitted and reinforced. The delay, Hitler believed, would give him time to regroup his forces behind the West Wall, Germany's belt of fortifications stretching north from Switzerland to the border of Holland. A resolute stand along the West Wall would give the Führer time to mount his master stroke.

Since the best defense could not fend off all his enemies indefinitely, Hitler decided to launch a major counteroffensive. The attack would strike with the force of those magnificent blitzkriegs that had won him most of Europe in 1939 and 1940. It would take the Western Allies by surprise and send their armies reeling back in defeat. The Führer could then turn all his forces to the east and smash the next Russian offensive. If everything went according to plan, his enemies would then be forced to sue for peace.

HITLER'S MASTER STROKE

Hitler's plan was grandiose, reckless—brilliant. It caught the overconfident Americans and British totally unprepared; a major offensive seemed so far beyond the present capability of Germany that the possibility scarcely occurred to them—until the onslaught hit in the middle of December, leading to the epic struggle that became known, because of the way it bent back the American line, as the Battle of the Bulge.

When Hitler began mulling his plan late in July, he quickly drew some general conclusions. For one thing, absolute secrecy was essential to the success of any counteroffensive. The Führer, secretive and suspicious by nature, had become positively paranoid about security since July 20, when a time bomb had exploded in a room at the Wolf's Lair where he was holding a conference. Hitler had escaped with only superficial injuries, but because the bomb had been planted by an anti-Nazi officer, Lieut. Colonel Claus von Stauffenberg, the Führer leaped to the conclusion that the whole Army was plotting against him.

Hitler therefore decided that he would personally plan and command his counteroffensive, and he so informed his Chief of Operations Staff, General Alfred Jodl, and a few other trusted advisers. One of the Führer's devoted followers later said: "It was a crushing, perhaps superhuman, task, even for a superman." Nevertheless, even in discussion with his hand-picked advisers, Hitler avoided mentioning the specifics of his plan as it developed through August and early September.

A place for the counteroffensive had to be selected, and Hitler decided at an early date that the attack must be staged somewhere in the west. Italy, in the south, would not serve his purpose; the peninsula was so isolated that victory there would not have much of an effect on the fighting elsewhere. He ruled out the vast Eastern Front because an attack of the size he contemplated—about 30 divisions—would be swallowed up there without a trace. "The Russians had so many troops," General Jodl later explained, "that even if we succeeded in destroying 30 divisions, it would not have made any difference. On the other hand, if we destroyed 30 divisions in the west, it would amount to one third of the whole invasion army."

Hitler had another reason for choosing to attack in the west. He believed that the British and the Americans could not respond quickly to a sudden breakthrough. A counterplan would surely have to be thrashed out in London and Washington, and by the time orders reached the front, the German assault forces no doubt would be well on their way to victory. (As an inveterate meddler in military affairs, Hitler could hardly have imagined that the Supreme Commander of the Allied Expeditionary Force, General Dwight D. Eisenhower, was fully empowered by both governments to react to any emergency as he saw fit. When the attack came, U.S. Army Chief of Staff General George C. Marshall would confirm the arrangement in a statement to his planners: "We can't help Eisenhower in any other way than not bothering him.")

Hitler had several sectors of the fast-changing Western Front under consideration as strike points for his offensive. He finally decided in early September to attack through the Ardennes region of Belgium and Luxembourg. The Ardennes—the classic invasion route taken by German armies in 1914 and 1940—was admittedly a region of difficult terrain: dense woodlands and rolling hills slashed by deep valleys and rugged ravines. But the Germans had occupied the region for four years before evacuating it in early September, and the commanders were familiar with the twists and turns in the vital roads that would speed the panzer divisions on their way.

Well before he decided to attack in the Ardennes, the Führer came to grips with the enormous problems of mustering the men and matériel for his offensive. He realized that his country would be strained to the utmost by the effort. In five years of warfare, the German Army had lost 3,360,000 men killed, wounded or missing, and the cruelest month of all, the August just past, had added 466,000 casualties. Some of the finest German units had been skeletonized by attrition: The proud Panzer Lehr (Tank Demonstration)—originally a division of 17,200 men and 190 tanks—now reported a total strength of two companies, some stragglers and five tanks; and the 2nd SS Panzer Division, which had once consisted of 20,000 men and 238 tanks, had been reduced to 2,650 men and a single serviceable tank. The Luftwaffe had been so severely reduced by attrition that it could not make a substantial contribution to the attack. German cities were piled with rubble. War industries, communications, rail lines and highway transport were constantly being disrupted by Allied bombing.

To solve the manpower problem, Hitler had inaugurated a series of drastic programs in August. He assigned Propaganda Minister Joseph Goebbels the task of combing all surplus workers out of business and industry. Goebbels announced that the length of the Reich's official work week would increase to 60 hours, that schools and theaters would be closed, that government bureaus would be stripped of nonessential personnel.

The Wehrmacht was ordered to eliminate noncombat jobs wherever possible. Administrative and logistical staffs and troops—"rear area swine," Hitler called them—were to be rooted out ruthlessly. All men between 16 and 60 years of age were declared eligible for military service (the previous range had been 18 to 50), and many airmen and sailors, who had been idled by the heavy losses of planes and ships, were to be transferred to the Army.

Most of the younger able-bodied men produced from all these sources were to form 25 new divisions, which Hitler named *Volksgrenadiers,* or people's infantry. Each of these units was considerably smaller than earlier German infantry divisions had been—only 10,000 men instead of 17,000. To offset the discrepancy, more men than usual were equipped with automatic weapons, including the rapid-firing burp guns—so called by the Americans because of the ripping *b-r-r-r-p* sound that they made. The German soldiers were also issued large numbers of *Panzerfausts*—hand-launched, rocket-firing antitank weapons.

In addition to the Volksgrenadiers, Hitler created 10 new panzer brigades, each built around a core of 40 tanks. These units were given top priority in the distribution of the new medium Panther tanks and the heavy Tiger tanks, which were now coming off the production lines in record numbers despite the Allied air raids. Parts of these panzer units, along with many of the Volksgrenadier divisions, would be used in the counteroffensive.

Finally, Hitler ordered the formation of about 100 "fortress" battalions. These infantry units were to be made up of older men and presumably would be of low fighting quality. They were assigned to the fortifications of the West Wall (where many of the units later rendered good service).

By early September all these programs had been put into

The Allies had reconquered most of northwestern Europe (shaded area) by September 16, 1944, when Hitler committed the Third Reich to a massive counteroffensive aimed at a large section (box) of Belgium and Luxembourg. At the time, six Allied armies faced an equal number of German armies along a 450-mile line from the North Sea to the Swiss border, including a portion of Hitler's 400-mile West Wall defense system.

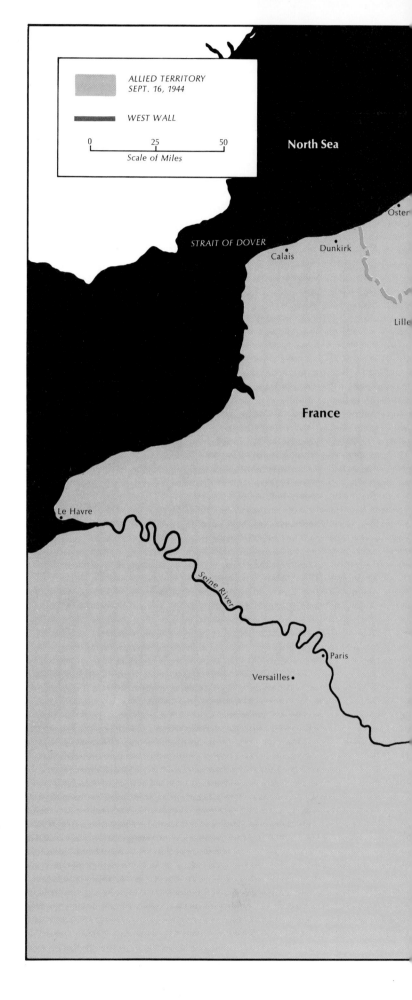

ALLIED TERRITORY
SEPT. 16, 1944

WEST WALL

0   25   50
Scale of Miles

North Sea

Oster

STRAIT OF DOVER

Calais   Dunkirk

Lille

France

Le Havre

Seine River

Paris

Versailles •

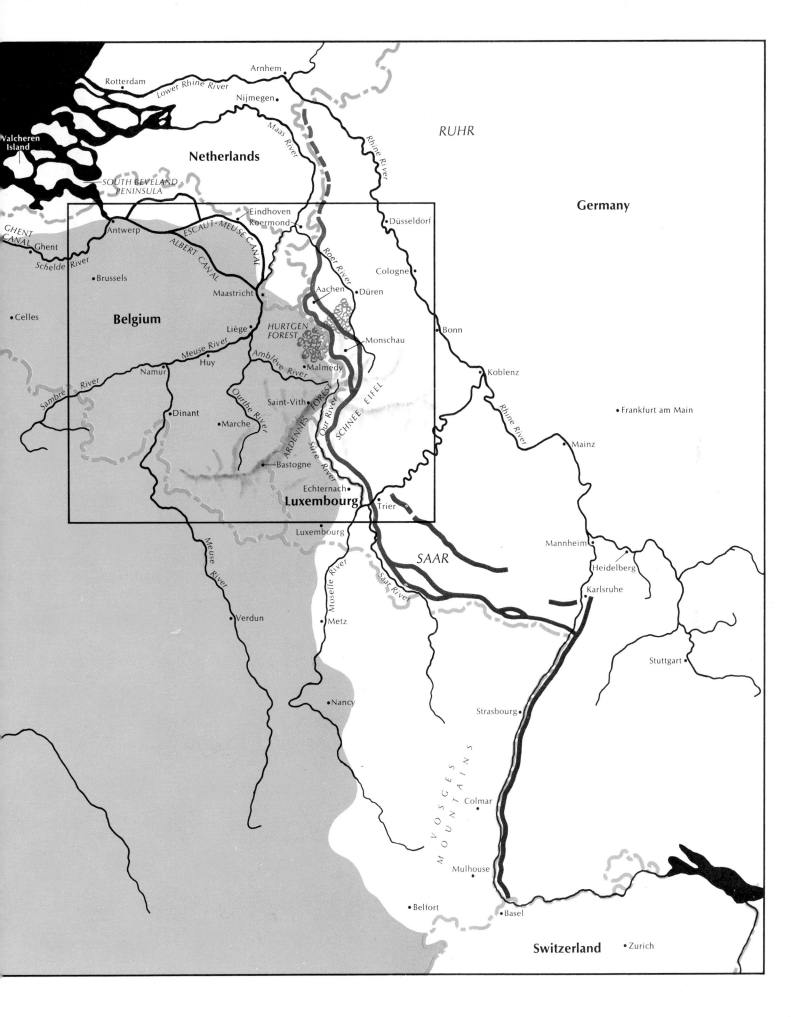

motion, and Hitler was considering ways of secretly withdrawing veteran panzer divisions from the Eastern Front to bolster his inexperienced attack force. The Führer kept his own counsel through the early days of September. But he had developed the plan as far as he could alone. To implement the training of his troops and the tactical planning of the offensive, he would soon have to take other people into his confidence.

The time arrived on September 16. As usual, Hitler came from his quarters to attend the daily briefing, and also as usual, visiting officers and officials who had not seen him recently were shocked by his appearance. According to the Führer's official diary keeper, Major Percy E. Schramm, Hitler "had suddenly grown old, his complexion looked unhealthy, he often stared vacantly, his back was bent, and his shoulders sunken, as if an invisible weight was crushing him. The most frightening impression, however, resulted from the tremble of his hands, which had become more pronounced during the last few months."

Most Führer watchers mistakenly blamed his condition on the Stauffenberg bomb plot, but a few insiders had guessed the bizarre cause of Hitler's wretched health. He was being treated for chronic stomach cramps by Dr. Theodor Morell, a charlatan who manufactured pharmaceuticals on the side and liked to try out his products on his patients. Recently

Morell had been supplying the Führer with large quantities of a patent medicine containing strychnine and belladonna. And Hitler, a notorious hypochondriac, was gulping so many of the pills that he was slowly poisoning himself.

The briefing turned up "nothing in particular," according to one attending general, Werner Kreipe, chief of staff of the Luftwaffe. But in view of what happened next, something in the battle reports might well have persuaded Hitler to commit himself irrevocably to the counteroffensive. Perhaps reports of American troops attacking in strength to either side of the Ardennes gave him reason to think that the Ardennes front would be thinly defended.

In any case, as the briefing broke up, Hitler called four of his top military advisers to a special meeting. They were General Jodl, General Kreipe, Field Marshal Wilhelm Keitel, chief of the high command of the Wehrmacht, and General Heinz Guderian, acting chief of staff of the Army, with special responsibilities for operations on the Eastern Front.

At the conference, Hitler asked Jodl for his latest assessment of the forces fighting on the Western Front. The operations chief noted that the German Army had 55 divisions on the line, as opposed to 96 for the Allies; he then launched into a discussion of the problems being encountered by German forces retreating from southern France.

Suddenly Hitler cut Jodl short, then lapsed into a long,

thoughtful silence. The generals, accustomed to the Führer's moods and theatrical displays, waited quietly for minutes. Then Hitler dropped his bombshell.

"I have just made a momentous decision," the Führer said. "I shall go over to the counterattack!" He jabbed his finger at the map on the table before him. "Here, out of the Ardennes, with the objective—Antwerp!"

While the generals sat stunned by the announcement, Hitler rushed on excitedly to explain his plan. A powerful German attack group, including some of the new Volksgrenadier divisions, would break through the thin shell of American defenders in the Ardennes and race across the Meuse River to capture the Belgian port, which had been occupied by the British on September 4. The bold thrust to Antwerp would split the American and the British armies, isolating the British in the north and driving them to the sea in "another Dunkirk." There was no need to fear the Allies' alleged advantage in strength; Jodl exaggerated.

Hitler raced on. He said that the Wehrmacht would need six to eight weeks to mount the offensive, and that in this period German forces would have to hold their current positions "under any condition" on a long line from the West Wall at the Swiss border to the Schelde Estuary on the North Sea in Holland. Hitler did not say so, but it was clear that by holding the Schelde the Germans would prevent the Allies from shipping much-needed supplies 60 miles upstream to Antwerp. German divisions on other fronts would stop all enemy attacks. They would receive no reinforcements, but certain panzer units might be transferred from the Eastern Front to add weight to the Ardennes assault.

At this point General Guderian protested. The withdrawal of divisions from the Russian front, he said, could lead to disaster there. Hitler brushed the objection aside.

Jodl too saw a problem. The Allies' overwhelming air superiority, he said, would jeopardize the counteroffensive. Hitler dismissed that point as well; the Luftwaffe, he replied, would supply 1,500 planes to cover the attack. The generals were astonished by that casual assumption. Such a force, ventured Kreipe, could not possibly be assembled. Hitler responded to that logic by disparaging the Luftwaffe, one of his favorite targets in recent weeks. Nothing would move him; he finally waved aside the danger of air assault by pointing out that the German attack would be launched in November; the usual bad weather, he said, would ground the Allies' air forces.

Jodl warned that intelligence reports indicated the strong possibility of an Allied airborne assault in Holland, which might disrupt the Führer's plan. Hitler ignored him.

The offensive, said the Führer, would be led by Field Marshal Gerd von Rundstedt. That distinguished officer had been removed as Commander in Chief West after the debacle in France. But his talents and prestige were needed to revive the broken German armies, and the Führer had recalled him to his old post early in September.

Finally Hitler swore his generals to secrecy. They were put under strict orders to bring only the most trustworthy subordinates into the planning, and as few of them as possible. The generals departed to breathe life into the Führer's grand design.

As Hitler's plan was developing in the first half of September, the Allies reached a strategic crossroads. Their breakneck advance toward Germany was in some ways just as disorderly as the Germans' retreat. The Allied supply situation was, as Hitler had anticipated, a matter of growing concern. By the time British and American units reached the West Wall, their supply lines were some 350 miles long, reaching all the way back to Normandy. Ports closer to the front line were denied the Allies by stubborn German resistance and extensive demolitions. Though the superb port of Antwerp had fallen intact into British hands on September 4, German forces downstream on both banks of the Schelde Estuary still blocked Allied shipping.

On September 5, General Eisenhower had written to the British commanding officer, Field Marshal Sir Bernard L. Montgomery, that opening Antwerp harbor was essential. But Montgomery was intent on making a deep thrust into Germany, in hopes of bringing the War to an end quickly: he did not want to weaken his attack by diverting units to clear Antwerp. On September 10 he countered with a plan for an Allied airborne assault—the very attack that General Jodl was later to refer to. Three airborne divisions would overleap the German forces retreating across Holland, secure a bridgehead on the far side of the Lower Rhine River and outflank the northern end of the West Wall. The plan, said Montgomery, would open the way into Germany.

Field Marshal Gerd von Rundstedt, at his desk at Western Front headquarters, did little more than sit there as the figurehead leader of the Ardennes offensive, which was planned and commanded by Hitler himself. Yet Rundstedt's reputation for conservative strategy made an advance contribution of sorts to the Germans: Allied planners expected only careful defensive operations in the west, and they were totally unprepared for Hitler's massive—and extremely risky—attack, which they referred to, ironically, as "the Rundstedt offensive."

There were powerful reasons for accepting Montgomery's plan. An Allied intelligence report issued early in September declared that the German Army is "no longer a cohesive force, but a number of fugitive battle groups, disorganized and even demoralized, short of equipment and arms." The mood of the Allies was optimistic, even exultant, and a number of commanders agreed with Montgomery that Germany could indeed be knocked out of the War by the end of the year.

So Eisenhower authorized Montgomery to execute his airborne assault, code-named Operation *Market-Garden*. The Allied airborne divisions—the British 1st and the U.S. 82nd and 101st—landed in three clusters in northern Holland on September 17, just a day after Hitler announced his attack plan. From there they set out to seize seven bridges and hold them until a strong relief force drove overland from the south.

Montgomery's daring scheme was thwarted by circumstance. Two panzer divisions had just been sent to the area for rehabilitation. Rundstedt buttressed this stroke of luck by a brilliant move. As the Allies raced north, he ordered

86,000 Germans of the Fifteenth Army, who had retreated from the northern coast of France, to be ferried across the Schelde Estuary. In this way they were able to escape eastward along a narrow neck of land and to remain intact as a fighting force opposing the Allied troops.

Thus it was that strong German forces turned up in northern Holland, where Montgomery had anticipated no great resistance. The Germans blocked the Allies' armored relief force and left the British 1st Airborne Division far out on the end of a limb. Before the British paratroopers were rescued, three quarters of their 10,000 men were dead, wounded or missing.

To General Eisenhower, the disastrous failure of *Market-Garden* meant two things. First, there was no longer a reasonable possibility of ending the war in Europe in 1944. Second, since the Allies were unlikely to launch the final assault on Germany until the spring of 1945, their forces would have to be supported through the winter with supplies from a source closer than Normandy. Therefore, Eisenhower directed Montgomery to clear the German defenders out of the Schelde Estuary and open the port of Antwerp.

The British commander assigned the task to the Canadian First Army, on the British left flank.

The Canadians launched their campaign on October 2, attacking across flooded terrain along both banks of the Schelde. The going was rough, and the Canadians made only slow progress. It soon became obvious to Eisenhower that larger forces had to be committed to the campaign, and he told Montgomery to use whatever troops were needed to do the job promptly.

Reluctantly, Montgomery diverted the British XII Corps from his attack toward Germany and sent it to support the right flank of the Canadians' attack. Eventually he also sent two British Commando forces on amphibious assaults that cracked the Germans' last stronghold on Walcheren Island. Yet the waterway to Antwerp was still barred by German mines. Not until the end of November did Allied ships begin delivering supplies to Antwerp. The Schelde campaign cost Montgomery 13,000 men killed, wounded and missing in action.

In the meantime, the Allies resorted to drastic measures to alleviate the supply shortage. A trucking line known as the Red Ball Express had been set up in August, and in the three months following, the drivers, mostly black members of the U.S. Quartermaster Corps, shuttled back and forth in long convoys, delivering more than 400,000 tons of matériel from Normandy to the front lines. An emergency airlift added nearly 1,000 tons daily. But the supplies were not nearly enough to support current needs, much less an all-out offensive.

In the early Allied attacks on the West Wall, the supply shortages caught up with one unit after another. Fuel for tanks and trucks was scarce. So was ammunition. Some outfits lacked the flamethrowers and explosives they needed to blast their way through the fortifications. There was no room in the truck convoys for winter clothing; with cold and snow coming on, the troops still wore the lightweight outfits provided for the June landing in Normandy. Even food was in short supply, and strict rationing had to be imposed. Some units supplemented their combat rations with captured stockpiles of German food.

As a result of the supply shortages and stiffening German resistance, the entire front stabilized gradually during late September and early October. In the north was Montgom-ery's Twenty-first Army Group, attempting to circle the West Wall and attack Germany's vital industrial Ruhr. Approaching the southern end of the West Wall was U.S. Lieut. General Jacob L. Devers' Sixth Army Group. And in the middle of the line was U.S. Lieut. General Omar N. Bradley's Twelfth Army Group, covering 200 miles of front between the French town of Epinal and Maastricht in Holland. On Bradley's southern flank Lieut. General George S. Patton's Third Army was attacking the fortifications around the city of Metz. The rest of Bradley's sector—including the Ardennes front earmarked by Hitler for his counteroffensive—was held by Lieut. General Courtney H. Hodges' First Army.

On October 2, General Hodges launched a limited offensive intended to penetrate the West Wall and capture the ancient city of Aachen. The XIX Corps would circle down toward Aachen and link up there with the VII Corps coming up from the south.

Bradley had prepared carefully for this renewed attack. He had rationed his scant supplies according to the work his armies would do; Hodges' First Army got 5,400 tons a day, while Patton's Third Army, which was being used in a secondary role, got 3,100 tons daily. And to free the two corps of the First Army for the attack, Bradley bolstered the central Ardennes front by moving up the small, newly organized U.S. Ninth Army.

The first part of the offensive, XIX Corps's attack on the West Wall toward Aachen, was to be preceded by a pulverizing 432-plane bombardment. But once again, as bitter experience in Normandy had already demonstrated, the tricky business of coordinating air attacks and ground assaults led to disaster. The 360 medium bombers failed to locate their targets, a number of road junctions. One group bombed a Belgian town 28 miles from the target area, killing 34 civilians and wounding at least 45. The 72 fighter-bombers managed to find their targets, the West Wall pillboxes, but scored not a single hit.

To make up for the failure of aerial bombardment, the XIX Corps commander, Major General Charles H. Corlett, took the risk of using the bulk of his rationed artillery ammunition, putting off until later any concern about replenishing the supply. In a 12-hour period nearly 19,000 artillery rounds were fired. Even so, the men of the assault

Rows of concrete "dragon's teeth"—the antitank barriers of Germany's West Wall, or Siegfried Line—zigzag across open farmland and past a road guarded by a steel gate. Spread out from 200 to 400 yards behind these obstacles were concealed pillboxes with overlapping fields of fire, troop shelters and command posts. This defensive system was designed to slow down an enemy assault until reserves could mount a counterattack.

force ran into rough going when they hit the West Wall. Casualties were heavy as the GIs pushed through the fortifications with flamethrowers, bazookas, pole charges, tanks and tank destroyers.

After five days and 1,800 casualties, XIX Corps troops were still three miles from the village where they were supposed to link up with the VII Corps. The last three miles proved to be the hardest for both attacking forces. The German High Command hurled two divisions of panzers and infantry into the battle, and it took nine more days of heavy fighting before the linkup could be effected.

With the ring finally closed, the reduction of Aachen could proceed. But the city had a special meaning for the Germans, and they were determined to hold it as long as possible. Aachen had been the seat of the Holy Roman Empire for more than five centuries. Charlemagne was born there and 32 subsequent emperors and kings were crowned at Aachen—and Hitler regarded himself as their successor.

Under orders from the Führer, Rundstedt told the commander at Aachen that he was to hold the venerable city to the last man; if necessary he must allow himself to be buried under its wreckage.

When the VII Corps closed in on Aachen, its vanguard 1st Division found the city in ruins. British bombers had pounded it so heavily that the streets were piled with rubble, and all but 20,000 of its 165,000 inhabitants had been evacuated. On October 11, Allied planes struck Aachen again, plastering targets on the edge of the city. Artillery then dumped 10,000 rounds on Aachen in two days.

After the bombardments, 1st Division troops were able to clear the Germans out of factories on the edge of Aachen. They entered the city on October 13 and worked their way through the rubble-filled streets. Covered by tanks and tank destroyers, the infantrymen inched forward, methodically rooting enemy troops out of storm sewers and cellars with flamethrowers, demolition charges and grenades.

A distraught German woman fights back tears as she prepares to evacuate Aachen, the first sizable German city captured by the Americans. Many citizens had stayed on in their homes despite Hitler's orders, issued on September 14, to abandon the place. They survived six weeks of Allied siege, living in gloomy cellars and subsisting on stored food and rain water. With Aachen in ruins, they finally departed for a safe area to the rear.

Two German divisions tried in vain to break through to assist the defenders.

On October 21, after eight days of bitter fighting, Aachen fell to the 1st Division, the first major German city to be captured by the Allies. But it was an empty prize. "The city is as dead as a Roman ruin," said an American intelligence report. "Burst sewers, broken gas mains, and dead animals have raised an almost overpowering smell in many parts of the city. The streets are paved with shattered glass; telephone, electric light and trolley cables are dangling and netted together everywhere, and in many places wrecked cars, trucks, armored vehicles and guns litter the streets."

With Aachen in Allied hands, and with the supply situation showing signs of improvement as quartermasters and engineers labored around the clock, the stage was set for the main effort of the offensive—the drive to the Roer River, to be followed by the crossing of the Cologne plain to the Rhine. The U.S. Ninth Army was moved north to attack on the left flank of Hodges' First Army. Far to the south, Patton's Third Army would attack toward the Saar, and Devers' Sixth Army Group would push forward to the Upper Rhine.

On the First Army front, four divisions of the VII Corps would make the main attack. But first, to protect the right flank of the drive, General Hodges ordered an attack into the region to the south known as Hürtgen Forest; otherwise, German units might assemble there under cover and swoop down to attack the Americans on the flank. It would be no easy task to clear the forest; the 9th Division had been trying to do just that since early October and had lost 4,500 men in the process. Now the 28th Division was assigned to fight its way through the Hürtgen region and take the key village of Schmidt, commanding a strategic ridge at the far side of the forest.

The attack was launched on November 2 after an artillery preparation of 11,000 rounds. The 28th Division soon came under intense machine-gun and small-arms fire. Germans seemed to be everywhere.

The men of the 28th thereupon learned what the 9th Division had discovered in October at such a terrible cost: Hürtgen Forest was a chamber of horrors, combining the most difficult elements of warfare, weather and terrain. Here, in a belt of rolling woodland 20 miles long and 10 miles deep, pillboxes of the West Wall nestled in the gloom among fir trees up to 100 feet tall. The forest was broken —but hardly relieved—by woodland trails, deep gorges carved by icy streams and high, swampy meadows with names like Deadman's Moor.

The advancing soldiers, held in the dark embrace of the forest, fought for survival. The Germans were well prepared, dug in behind bunkers and log-covered foxholes. At any moment, a GI might walk into a burst of bullets from a hidden machine gun, or lose his legs in the blast of a mine ingeniously encased in wood or plastic to foil metal mine detectors. If a man dived for cover in a ditch or an abandoned foxhole, he might trip a wire and be buried by an explosion. He might be killed if he stopped to aid an injured comrade. One badly wounded GI, diabolically booby-trapped by the Germans, lay motionless for 72 hours, fighting pain, delirium and unconsciousness so that he could tell

Two grim-faced German youths, captured while attempting to ambush GIs from a wooded area near Aachen, are marched away by an American MP for questioning. The boys, aged 14 (left) and 10, had been trained to be snipers by the local chapter of the Hitler Youth.

rescuers about the bomb. He was finally found by medics; on his warning, they disconnected the booby trap before administering lifesaving first aid.

For many of the soldiers the worst of all the horrors was the helpless exposure to "tree bursts," artillery shells that screamed in among the lofty pines, exploding on trunks and branches and spraying a rain of splintery death over a wide area below. When a man threw himself flat on the ground, he only made himself a bigger target for a tree burst.

In spite of tough early going, one battalion of the 28th Division slipped into Schmidt on the second day of the attack. It seemed too good to be true, and it was. On the morning of November 4, German tanks launched a counterattack. The GIs had nothing but bazookas to stop the attack, and the rockets bounced harmlessly off the heavily armored Panther tanks. As the Panthers bore down on Schmidt, panic swept through the ranks of the U.S. battalion. The men fled to the village of Kommerscheidt, where another battalion tried to stop them, threatening them with pistols and wrestling with them. It took an hour and a half to corral some 200 men to set up a defense there.

Three days later, disaster struck. In a bitter cold rain, 15 German tanks and an infantry battalion hit the Americans at Kommerscheidt, overran the foxholes occupied by some soldiers and buried the men in knee-deep mud. Those who could ran for the woods to the north, and others surrendered. After that, it was all downhill for the 28th Division. By mid-November, the 28th was so badly chewed up that it was relieved and sent to the quiet Ardennes front for rest and rehabilitation. It was replaced in Hürtgen Forest by the 8th Division; then the 8th too was badly mauled.

At about the same time that the 8th Division entered the Hürtgen battle, the First Army launched its main attack to the north. The drive toward the Rhine north of the forest jumped off on November 16, preceded by the largest aerial preparation attempted up to that point. A total of 2,800 heavy and medium bombers dumped more than 10,000 tons of bombs on target areas in the zone of advance. The artillery preparation was just as spectacular. Nearly 700 guns fired more than 50,000 rounds.

In spite of the shattering bombardments, the Germans managed to pull themselves together, and the breakthrough anticipated by Allied commanders turned out to be a slugging match. It took two infantry regiments four days and more than 1,000 casualties to push forward about two miles. An armored combat command lost 50 per cent of its infantry and 42 of its 64 medium tanks while grinding forward through open country to the east of Aachen. Not until December 16 did VII Corps troops reach the Roer River, and then only at the cost of heavy casualties.

In the meantime, the battle for Hürtgen Forest went on and on, constantly demanding more and more new troops. A regiment of the 1st Division took a pounding in the northern fringe of the forest. The 4th Division suffered such heavy losses that, like the 28th, it was pulled out and sent to the quiet Ardennes front for repairs. Then the 83rd Division was sent into the deadly forest, followed in turn by the 5th Armored and several smaller special units. It was as if the battle had become an end in itself and the American commanders had been hypnotized into making endless sacrifices.

Unit after unit, green troops and veterans alike, moved through the killing ground in a kind of endless, slow-motion nightmare. Private George Barrette, a radio operator, later said of his first artillery barrage: "Me and this buddy of mine were in the same hole with only a little brush on top, and I remember I was actually bawling. We were both praying to the Lord over and over again to please stop the barrage. We were both shaking and shivering and crying and praying all at the same time.

"They sent me back to an aid station for a while and I guess they treated me for shock or something. Then they sent me back to my outfit. Everything was just as cold and slimy as it was before and the fog so thick you couldn't see 15 yards away."

Barrette returned to another artillery barrage. "It was the same shells, the same goddamn shells," he said. "Soon as I got there the Jerries started laying them on again. They started laying them all over the road and I tried to dig in and then I started shaking and crying again. I guess I must have banged my head against a tree or something because I lost my senses. I couldn't hear anything. I don't remember exactly what happened but I was walking down the road and I remember seeing this soldier crawling out of a tank with both arms shot off. I remember helping him

Advancing through the dangerous Hürtgen Forest, mud-splattered infantrymen of the U.S. 4th Division clamber out of a gulch clotted with barbed wire, felled trees and other debris. American GIs frequently lobbed grenades or small charges of TNT ahead of them in order to set off any mines or booby traps that German soldiers might have placed in their path.

and then I don't remember any more, I guess I must have gone off my nut."

The number of soldiers who lost their minds or their nerve was a good index to the sheer savagery of the fighting. Veterans cracked under the strain; a company commander and one of his platoon leaders, who had seen their men chopped down by machine guns, mines and artillery fire, "just went berserk, crying and yelling," a sergeant recalled. In four days three company commanders lost their commands for failing to advance. In another company, all the officers either broke down or were relieved, and one platoon leader who refused to order his men back into action was placed under arrest.

As the battle raged, the forest became a scene that "only the devil himself could have created." So said the official history of the battle, written by Charles B. MacDonald, who fought in the area as a rifle-company commander. "Once-magnificent trees were now twisted, gashed, broken, their limbs and foliage forming a thick carpet on the floor of the forest. Some trees stood like gaunt, outsized toothpicks.

Great jagged chunks of concrete and twisted reinforcing rods that together had been a pillbox. The mutilated carcass of a truck that had hit a mine. Everywhere discarded soldier equipment—gas masks, empty rations containers, helmets, rifles, here a field jacket with a sleeve rent, there a muddy overcoat with an ugly clotted dark stain on it. One man kicked a bloody shoe from his path, then shuddered to see that the shoe still had a foot in it. . . . Here and there the bodies of the dead lay about in grotesque positions, weather-soaked, bloated, the stench from them cloying."

All told, 120,000 men and additional thousands of replacements were fed into the Hürtgen meat grinder. Finally, on December 13, units of the 83rd Infantry and 5th Armored Divisions broke into the open at two little villages on the far side of the forest. By then, more than 24,000 American soldiers had been reported killed, wounded, captured or missing in action, and another 9,000 had fallen victim to disease or battle fatigue. More than 25 per cent of the Americans who fought in Hürtgen Forest were casualties.

Six German divisions plus parts of two others—a total of

more than 80,000 men—had suffered losses of approximately the same order. But they had covered themselves with glory. They had bought time, precious time, for other Germans to ready the Ardennes attack.

In the fall, the Germans' defense had changed radically in character and spirit. Gone was the desperation of September, when the troops were panic-stricken and commanders wildly juggled understrength units to plug up holes in the lines. Gone too was the grim pessimism that gripped officers and men even when the line was stabilized. By November units all along the front were standing to fight, and when they retreated they did so in good order, after exacting a heavy toll. In December the German Army was once again a formidable fighting force.

The Germans called the resurgence of their Army "the Miracle of the West," and the claim hardly seemed exaggerated. But the Germans remained under extreme pressure everywhere, and commanders were constantly begging higher headquarters for reinforcements and matériel. Their appeals got them nowhere, for reasons known only to the select few Hitler had entrusted with organizing his Ardennes counteroffensive. As late as the third week of October, Field Marshal von Rundstedt had not been told of the attack he was supposed to command. Neither had Field Marshal Walther Model, commander of Army Group B, whose troops would execute the Ardennes offensive.

On October 22 Hitler was finally ready to draw these generals into his plan, and he summoned their chiefs of staff to his Wolf's Lair headquarters. Rundstedt's chief, Lieut. General Siegfried Westphal, and Model's chief, Lieut. General Hans Krebs, had no idea of the purpose of the meeting but planned to seize the opportunity to ask for more troops to prevent an Allied breakthrough to the Rhine.

On their arrival both generals were vastly encouraged by a paper handed them, listing 13 infantry divisions, two parachute divisions and six panzer-type divisions that would be arriving on the Western Front in late November and early December. Then they were sworn to secrecy on pain of death and led into a meeting with the Führer, Field Marshal Keitel and a few others.

Hitler astonished the two chiefs of staff with his plan for the Ardennes offensive. They were astonished again when the Führer told them that none of the divisions on the list could be used in defense. Instead of being given reinforcements, Westphal and Krebs were told that they would contribute three infantry divisions and six panzer divisions from the Western Front to the Ardennes offensive.

The Führer promised that 1,500 planes would be available for the attack, reaffirming his original statement on September 16. Included in that number, he said, would be 100 brand-new jets. Keitel added that 4,250,000 gallons of gasoline and 50 trainloads of ammunition would also be set aside for the offensive.

Westphal and Krebs returned to their headquarters and briefed Rundstedt and Model. Rundstedt called the plan a "stroke of genius," but he said it was entirely too ambitious for the force at hand. Model was less tactful when he learned the news. "This plan hasn't got a damned leg to stand on," he said.

Together, Rundstedt and Model worked out a more modest plan for destroying Allied divisions in the Aachen sector. Their small plan was later presented to Hitler, but he rejected it in favor of his own "big solution." Rundstedt was informed of the Führer's reaction by Jodl, who admitted the risks in the Ardennes undertaking. "In our present situation, however," said Jodl, "we must not shrink from staking everything on one card."

Hitler's daring gamble went forward, and to prevent the Allies from getting wind of it, an elaborate deception was contrived. The offensive was given the code name *Watch on the Rhine* to convey the impression that it was an operation designed to defend the great river barrier. To lend realism to the deception, part of the attack force was assembled in the Rheydt-Jülich-Cologne area, east of Aachen, where it would be in position to prevent Allied crossings of the Rhine. Here, military preparations were carried out ostentatiously and radio traffic was conspicuously increased. Additional antiaircraft units were brought into the area to thicken flak concentrations and to draw the attention of Allied pilots to the forces there.

In the meantime, the main body of troops was assembled opposite the Ardennes. Here, the strictest security precautions were observed. Radio silence was enforced; tanks and other vehicles were heavily camouflaged. Severe limitations were placed on reconnaissance patrols and artillery activity

Four important weapons used by the Germans in the Ardennes offensive appear at right. On the ground beside a German soldier's foxhole, an MP-44 automatic assault rifle and a newly developed G-43 semiautomatic rifle lie across a Panzerfaust, an antitank weapon similar to the U.S. bazooka. At far right, an American studies a captured Nebelwerfer, the five-barreled rocket launcher that the Germans used to supplement their conventional artillery. Its projectiles made a horrifying screeching noise that earned them the GI nickname "screaming meemies."

for fear that they would reveal the troop concentrations and tip off the impending attack.

The plan behind this elaborate scheme called for the force east of Aachen to move to the south under cover of night and join the main force just before the attack was launched. To add to the Allies' confusion, a dummy army was created in the Düsseldorf-Cologne area northeast of the force near Aachen. Small work parties appeared in the area; quarters were prepared for Army personnel, signposts were put up and radio traffic was initiated to give the impression a new defensive army was being formed there.

The problems involved in assembling the attack forces were enormous. Divisions had to be transported to the assembly areas from as far away as Austria, East Prussia and Denmark. Bridges over the Rhine, which had recently been prepared for demolition to prevent any Allied crossing to the east, now had to be buttressed to carry the heavy traffic in the opposite direction.

Movement to the assembly areas was mostly by rail. The trains, hidden in tunnels or forests during the day, moved at night to the appointed areas, unloaded swiftly and returned for another load before daylight. Air-raid warning stations were erected near assembly areas, and when Allied planes were reported heading that way, the trains were rushed into tunnels. So effective were the precautions that the German losses to Allied air attacks totaled only eight ammunition cars in September, 11 cars of ammunition and rations in October, and four cars of gasoline in November. In the month of November, the assembly areas received 3,982 carloads of ammunition, fuel, rations, horses, coal, weapons and equipment. Between September and December, the total was nearly 10,000 carloads, 144,735 tons of supplies.

Nevertheless, logistical problems forced Hitler to postpone his offensive several times. The original attack date, set at November 1 by Hitler, was moved up to November 25, then postponed successively to December 10, December 15 and finally December 16. The delays did not seem to matter greatly; bad weather was still predicted for mid-December, and postponements were not new to the High Command. The western blitzkrieg in 1940 had been postponed 16 times.

As the plan was finally worked out, four armies would be involved in the operation. The main attack force would be SS General Josef "Sepp" Dietrich's Sixth Panzer Army, which would break through the northern part of the Ardennes front, cross the Meuse River, then wheel northwest and head for Antwerp. To the south of Dietrich, Lieut. General Hasso von Manteuffel's Fifth Panzer Army would drive across the Meuse to Brussels and Antwerp, protecting the left flank of the Sixth. Lieut. General Erich Brandenberger's Seventh Army would protect the southern shoulder of the breakthrough area against Allied counterattack, and Lieut. General Günther Blumentritt's Fifteenth Army would do the same on the northern shoulder of the salient. Infantry units in the attacking armies would pave the way for the panzers by punching gaps in the American defenses at vital roadways running west.

To sow confusion and terror among American troops, Hitler personally organized a panzer brigade, to be led by Lieut. Colonel Otto Skorzeny, whose daredevil feats as a

commando prompted Allied intelligence to call him "the most dangerous man in Europe." Skorzeny's men were to be dressed in captured American uniforms and equipped with captured American tanks, jeeps, arms and identification. They were to race to the Meuse, seize several bridges, commit sabotage and generally create consternation in the Americans' rear areas.

In addition, a 1,000-man parachute force under Colonel Friedrich von der Heydte, a veteran of the German airborne assault on Crete, was to land behind the American lines, open roads for German armor and block enemy units from interfering with the panzers' progress.

To prevent detection by the Allies, all the units in the German offensive were to be held at least 12 miles from the front until Hitler gave the order for the final assembly. Then troops and tanks would move up on a rigid timetable.

Unit commanders received their final briefing in two groups on the nights of December 11 and 12. They assembled at Rundstedt's headquarters at Ziegenberg Castle near Frankfurt. There they were disarmed, then taken by bus over a circuitous route to a nearby bunker where the Führer had moved his headquarters in order to be near the Ardennes front. Known as the Eagle's Nest, the bunker had served as the command post for the blitzkrieg through the Ardennes in 1940.

The Führer himself received the commanders and electrified one group with a speech that lasted nearly two hours. He explained his attack scheme in detail and exhorted the men to a supreme effort. "This battle," he concluded, "is to decide whether we shall live or die. I want all my soldiers to fight hard and without pity. The battle must be fought with brutality, and all resistance must be broken in a wave of terror. The enemy must be beaten—now or never! Thus lives our Germany!"

On December 12, all units were alerted for movement. The following night they took up positions on a base line opposite the Ardennes, with the force assembled opposite Aachen slipping down from the north. To muffle the sound of traffic, wagon wheels and horses' hooves were padded with straw, and low-flying aircraft zoomed over the assembly areas to drown out engine noises. Charcoal was issued for fires so that woodsmoke would not betray the location of massed troops. Guns and howitzers were moved into position five miles behind the lines, and to cut down on noise and conserve gasoline, ammunition for the opening barrage was moved up by hand.

By the night of December 15, everything was in place for the counteroffensive. Opposite the Ardennes, 20 divisions were poised for the jump-off, with five more in reserve. Although Hitler had fallen slightly short of his goal of 30 divisions, he had mustered a powerful force of approximately 300,000 men, 1,900 pieces of artillery, and 970 tanks and armored assault guns.

The troops who would do the fighting were assembled by their officers on the night of December 15 and briefed on the operation. Then, in the freezing cold, they listened to an officer read a message from Rundstedt.

"Soldiers of the Western Front! Your great hour has come. Large attacking armies have started against the Anglo-Americans. I do not have to tell you more than that. You feel it yourself. We gamble everything! You carry with you the holy obligation to give all to achieve superhuman objectives for our Fatherland and our Führer!"

On the other side of the line, the Americans were completely ignorant of the German preparations. A general optimism lulled even normally apprehensive intelligence officers; it did not occur to them that the Germans had the wherewithal to mount a major counteroffensive. On December 12, an intelligence summary issued by General Bradley's headquarters declared: "It is now certain that attrition is steadily sapping the strength of German forces on the western front and that the crust of defenses is thinner, more brittle and more vulnerable than it appears." The summary concluded that "the balance at present is in favor of the Allies. With continuing Allied pressure in the south and in the north, the breaking point may develop suddenly and without warning."

The top American commanders were preoccupied with attacks in other areas. The U.S. First and Ninth Armies were attacking in the Roer River area. The Third Army was attacking across the Saar, and the Sixth Army Group was closing in on the Rhine after capturing Strasbourg. The very few people who suggested that a German counteroffensive in the Ardennes was a remote possibility were humored by their companions. General Bradley, visiting the VIII Corps's commander, Major General Troy H. Middleton, at his headquarters in Bastogne, was surprised to hear Middleton say that the long front assigned to him in the Ardennes was too thinly held. "Don't worry, Troy," said Bradley, "they won't come through here."

But the Ardennes front was indeed thinly held. Deployed along the 85-mile sector were a lightly armed cavalry group, an armored division and four infantry divisions, two of them green and the other two exhausted. The green divisions were the 99th, which had been deployed in the northern part of the Ardennes for five weeks but had seen little action, and the 106th, which had just arrived at the front on December 11. South of them were the 28th and 4th Divisions; both of these units had been worn out by the fighting in Hürtgen Forest and were in the Ardennes for rest and rehabilitation.

As the day of the counteroffensive neared, the Americans picked up a number of clues that something big was about to happen. Aerial reconnaissance noted increased vehicular traffic in the German assembly area. Long hospital trains were spotted on the west bank of the Rhine; flatcars bearing Tiger tanks were observed, and a general increase in motor traffic at night was reported. But the signs were misread by intelligence experts; they concluded that the Germans were probably moving units to the Aachen or Saar areas, which were threatened by American attacks.

Forward units of the 106th Division clearly heard the sound of motors on their front—despite the low-flying German aircraft. This information was reported to VIII Corps headquarters by the division commander, Major General Alan W. Jones. A staff officer told him: "Don't be so jumpy. The Krauts are just playing phonograph records to scare you newcomers." The 28th Division also noted increased vehicular traffic, but decided that it probably was caused by a routine relief of a German unit pulling out of the line.

A captured document had revealed the existence of Otto Skorzeny's special commando units, but not their mission. The respected Fifth and Sixth Panzer Armies were discovered to have been withdrawn from the northern sector of the front and could not be located on the map, but nothing was made of this development. Recently captured German prisoners of war displayed markedly high morale. But these and other clues were ignored, discounted or lost in the shuffle as the Allied armies went about their business.

One man in the intelligence apparatus was reasonably certain that something strange was up. He was Colonel Benjamin A. "Monk" Dickson, head of First Army intelligence. In a report issued on the 10th of December, Dickson noted that information had been obtained from an "extremely intelligent" prisoner of war. This man, "whose observations check exactly with established facts, stated that every means possible is being gathered for the coming all-out counteroffensive."

Dickson concluded that the attack would hit an area slightly north of the Ardennes. But then on December 14, Dickson read a report from a local woman saying that she had observed "many horse-drawn vehicles, pontoons, small boats and other river-crossing equipment coming from the direction of Bitburg, and moving toward Geichlingen."

The area she was speaking of lay opposite the Ardennes, just east of the sector held by the 28th Division. That night, Dickson told the First Army commander, General Hodges: "It's the Ardennes!" But Dickson was considered impetuous and a little overwrought. He needed a rest. The following morning, he went off for a four-day leave in Paris. He was there when the German armies struck in the Ardennes.

HAPPY DAYS IN THE ARDENNES

GIs on a three-day pass queue up to receive their billeting assignments at their division's rest center in the town of Clervaux, on the peaceful Ardennes front.

A RUSTIC VACATION FROM WAR

While German armies were preparing for their attack into the Ardennes, Americans stationed there were enjoying themselves greatly. All through the autumn of 1944, a halcyon mood pervaded the region: The GIs on combat duty spent much of their time playing poker, ogling pinup girls in *Yank* magazine, building dugouts or log cabins for their winter quarters and looking forward to a visit to a rest center. Periodically the soldiers were given a pass to one of the Army's dozen-odd rest areas in Luxembourg and Belgium, where they could enjoy three days of sport, relaxation and dates with the local women.

In each rest area, the Army maintained a recreation center amply equipped for fun and games. For example, the Vielsalm center—located in an old Belgian Army barracks—included a Red Cross club, an indoor rifle range, a GI barber shop that gave free shaves and haircuts, a movie theater and a gymnasium that went by the name of "Madison Square Garden." The big attractions, of course, were the neatly uniformed American Red Cross hostesses and the touring USO entertainers who put on shows in the gym.

Venturing out of the centers, GIs discovered pleasant pastimes everywhere. They meandered through the quaint towns and fashionable resorts of the region, buying souvenirs, and consuming great quantities of beer, ice cream and apple pie. "We were like kids," recalled a company commander, "excited with the slightest luxury." The Americans roamed the deep forests hunting deer and wild boar. (To the distress of the Luxembourg forest warden, some of the hunters took to shooting boar with submachine guns from low-flying observation planes.)

The Ardennes was, in short, a soldier's dream come true. Its peace and rustic delights blotted out the War, which seemed to be nearly over anyway. Like almost every GI in the Ardennes, Private Joe Schectman was content and optimistic. "We are billeted as comfortably and safely as we were in England," he wrote his parents on December 15. "Of course there's no telling how long I'll be in this paradise. But as long as I am, I'll be safe."

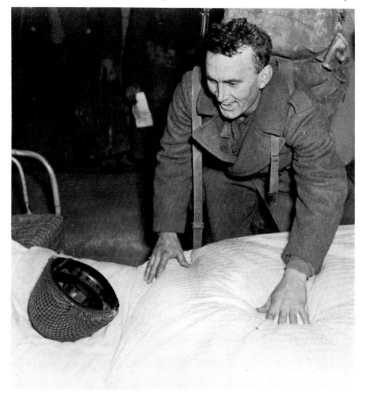

An ecstatic American soldier, newly arrived at a Luxembourg rest area, tests the soft bed and plump feather quilt that will be his for the next few days.

Wallowing blissfully, a sergeant signals his approval of his first bath in the famous warm mud of Spa, a Belgian resort also renowned for its mineral springs.

The touring U.S. Army Band puts on a concert for off-duty GIs and the inhabitants of Spa in October 1944. The less-august bands of divisions stationed in that

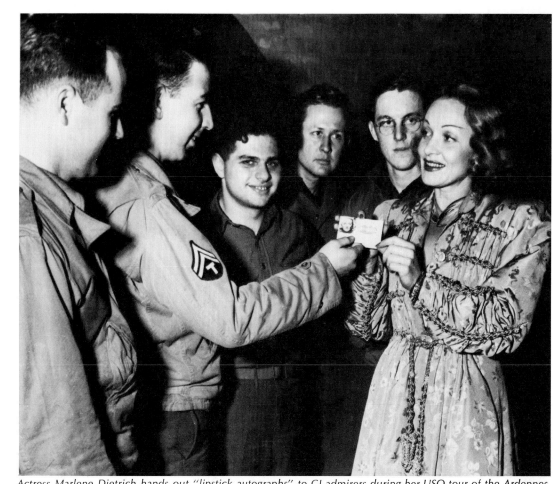

Actress Marlene Dietrich hands out "lipstick autographs" to GI admirers during her USO tour of the Ardennes.

area played suitable music for dances, variety shows and holiday dinners.

GIs and their Belgian dates find an Army beer garden's sign to their liking.

Frontline soldiers kill time shooting craps in a dugout in the Ardennes.

An infantryman takes a mighty cut during a baseball game between two units on leave in the Luxembourg town of Consthum.

GI sports fans at a rest center

in Saint-Vith wait out a pause in a reenactment of the annual Army-Navy game, won 23 to 7 by Army with heroics by its stars "Doc" Blanchard and Glenn Davis.

Rubbernecking medics watch while a Luxembourg couple operate a mobile woodcutting machine on a street in Wiltz.

A Belgian shopper in a Liège department store helps American soldiers select stuffed animals for the kids back home.

An American private of

the 1st Division bargains with an enterprising Belgian shopkeeper for wooden shoes, a favorite GI souvenir. His buddy inspects the pair he has just bought.

Army postal workers unload Christmas gifts from the U.S. in Belgium. But holiday cheer was destined to be in short supply. On December 16, three days after

Dressed as St. Nicholas, a GI hands out gifts to children in the Ardennes.

this photograph was taken, a great wave of German tanks and troops broke over the American lines, and the GIs' vacation from war gave way to nightmare.

2

Assault by "artificial moonlight"
"What are those damned Huns up to?"
A lone platoon holds the road at Lanzerath
Peiper's panzers burst into the clear
A trail of SS massacres
German commandos in GI disguise
A look-alike decoy for Ike
The fiasco of von der Heydte's airborne attack
Two U.S. divisions "skin the cat"
A defense line manned by cooks and clerks
Stymieing the panzers

At precisely 5:30 a.m. on December 16, 1944, an American sentry on the quiet Ardennes front telephoned his company headquarters with a strange report. Innumerable "pinpoints of light," he said, had suddenly begun flickering along the German line. An instant later, German shells crashed around him, and the observer realized that the lights were actually the muzzle flashes of hundreds of German guns. He was witnessing the opening salvo of the Battle of the Bulge.

All along the 85-mile front, from the medieval town of Echternach in the south to the cobblestoned honeymoon resort of Monschau in the north, American units were shaken from sleep by the thunderous artillery bombardment. Shells screamed in over the American positions, the ground trembled, trees were splintered and ugly black patches appeared in the six-inch blanket of snow. The shells came in all sizes—from mortars, multiple rocket launchers, howitzers, 88mm and 14-inch railway guns.

GIs leaped out of sleeping bags, grabbed their weapons and dived for foxholes. Platoon leaders and forward observers reached for field telephones; many discovered that their lines were dead, the wires cut by the shelling. Switching over to radios, they found their wavelengths jammed by the martial music of German bands.

At first, no one knew what to make of the shelling. Green troops thought it was "outgoing mail"—friendly fire. Even veterans were baffled; the meager German forces said to be holding the front could not manage such a heavy bombardment. In one sector where a grand total of two horse-drawn German guns had been reported, an officer made a grim quip: "They sure are working those horses to death."

After an hour or so, the shelling let up and the morning mists of the Ardennes were bathed in an eerie glow. The Germans had switched on giant searchlights, bouncing their powerful beams off low-hanging clouds to illuminate the American positions. German infantrymen advanced through this false dawn—spectral figures in snow-white camouflage suits or in mottled battle dress. In foxholes and concealed bunkers, GIs braced themselves for the attack.

At the southern end of the Ardennes front, the veterans of the 4th Infantry Division—which had suffered 6,000 casualties in the battle of Hürtgen Forest—fought with courage and skill; some 60 members of one company barricaded themselves in a hotel near Echternach to repel German

A WAVE OF TERROR

assaults. Elsewhere on the 4th Division's front, isolated outposts were either overrun or pushed back and surrounded by overwhelming pressure from enemy infantry.

Immediately to the north of the 4th Division, a battalion of the green 9th Armored Division had only recently been assigned a three-mile sector of the front to provide some limited patrolling and combat experience. But the sector had been so quiet that the 9th Armored commander was beginning to worry that his men would gain no experience at all. Awakened by a 1,000-round artillery barrage on the morning of the 16th, the armored infantrymen found themselves facing almost an entire German division. The enemy assault troops quickly infiltrated under cover of fog through the numerous ravines and gorges that cut across the forested and hilly terrain.

Farther north, in towns and villages along a scenic road the GIs had dubbed "Skyline Drive," infantrymen of the battered 28th Infantry Division, which had suffered more than 6,100 casualties in Hürtgen Forest, were surrounded in their positions while the main German tank units bypassed them and drove toward more important objectives—the towns of Clervaux and Bastogne.

North of the 28th Division's sector, on a long, high ridge known as the Schnee Eifel, the 106th Division was stunned by the sudden attack. The infantrymen of the 106th—recruits who had arrived on the front just five days earlier, without combat experience—had been told they were coming into a quiet sector, and instead they found themselves fighting for their lives. Everyone pitched in. Clerks, cooks and KPs joined the battle, and the division band rushed forward to guard the division headquarters at Saint-Vith.

In the Losheim Gap, a seven-mile pass on the northern edge of the Schnee Eifel, the attackers swept past scattered cavalry units of the 14th Cavalry Group, a battalion-sized, mechanized reconnaissance unit attached to the 106th Division. In the village of Manderfeld, streets were jammed with retreating troops, vehicles and artillery pieces. Some civilians begged to be taken along; others eagerly awaited the return of the Germans. There were signs of panic in the confusion and the haste to get out of the way. A cavalry colonel turned over his unit to his executive officer and headed for the rear.

The remainder of the Ardennes front, from the 106th Division's sector north to Monschau, was the responsibility of the 99th Infantry Division, another inexperienced outfit that had been on the line for little more than a month. The men of the 99th had known for some time that December 16 would be an exciting day: a USO troupe led by film actress Marlene Dietrich was scheduled to perform at division headquarters that morning. When the entertainers arrived, they were immediately rushed out of the danger zone; by that time the frontline GIs were receiving a bloody baptism of fire. At the northern end of the front, riflemen of the 99th were shooting enemy foot soldiers at such close range that the Germans toppled dead into the American foxholes. At the town of Losheimergraben, near the southern end of the 99th Division front, a mortarman set his weapon at an almost vertical angle and dropped shells on a German assault force barely 25 feet away. Nearby, GIs repelled repeated waves of German infantry but were finally overwhelmed by tanks, which crushed some of the Americans to death in their foxholes.

Even though GIs up and down the length of the 85-mile front were engaged in desperate combat that day, the general disruption of telephone communications led most of the American units to assume that the German attacks were purely local. Until the radio network began to function, companies were cut off from their battalions, battalions from their regiments, and regiments from their divisions. It was difficult for any of the field commanders to form a clear picture of what was going on.

Higher headquarters were even less informed than the isolated units. Nearly four hours after the German artillery had first opened up, General Bradley, commander of the Twelfth Army Group, left his headquarters at the Luxembourg capital bound for a meeting with the Supreme Commander, General Eisenhower, unaware that the Germans were attacking less than 20 miles away. At First Army headquarters in the resort of Spa, some 30 miles behind the front, General Hodges admitted that "the enemy line cannot be well defined as the front is fluid and somewhat obscure." Nearby, at Eupen, V Corps commander General Leonard T. Gerow was angry and uncertain. "What are those damned bastards of Huns up to?" he demanded of a member of his staff.

To cap the confusion that permeated the U.S. chain of

command, one unit was vigorously pushing forward even as the German units were beginning to break through American positions on either side: Three days earlier, the 2nd Infantry Division had thrust into German territory through a narrow corridor in the 99th Division's lines in an attempt to reach the Roer River *(map, below)*. The veteran outfit had finally captured a key road junction in the early morning hours of December 16 and was rushing more troops forward to exploit the penetration.

As fragmentary reports of German advances began to trickle into V Corps headquarters, General Gerow realized that the 2nd was in danger of being cut off and wiped out. On the afternoon of the 16th, he called First Army headquarters and asked General Hodges for permission to call off the attack. But Hodges still believed that the German

attacks were localized and was unwilling to abandon the 2nd Division's hard-won breakthrough. He ordered the soldiers to keep moving forward.

While uncertainty reigned in the American command, the fighting quickly turned into a series of small-unit actions. But one of these clashes, involving only 18 men of the U.S. 99th Division, would have a major impact on the course of the German offensive in the northern part of the front.

When Hitler's Great Blow fell, First Lieutenant Lyle J. Bouck Jr. and 17 men of his intelligence and reconnaissance platoon were at Lanzerath, a village in the strategic Losheim Gap. This natural thoroughfare through forested ridges and plateaus was only lightly defended by a 450-man unit of the 14th Cavalry Group, a reconnaissance unit. Recognizing the

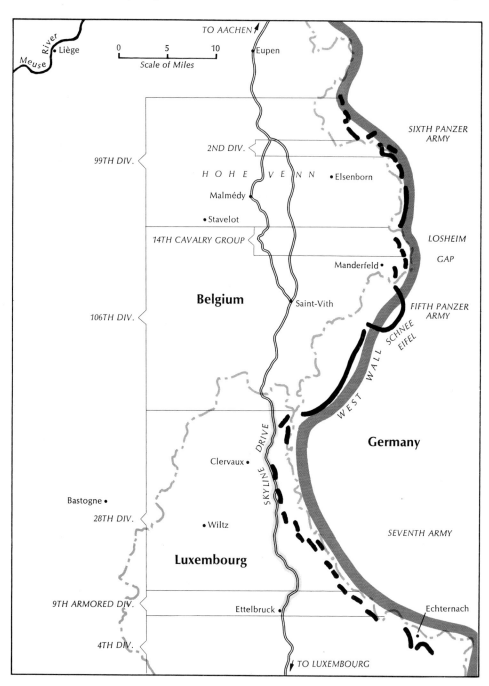

On December 16, 1944, more than 250,000 Germans attacked 83,000 American troops deployed thinly along the 85-mile Ardennes front (broken line). In the north, the Sixth Panzer Army struck the U.S. 99th Division and threatened to cut off the U.S. 2nd Division, attacking into Germany through the West Wall. In the center, the Fifth Panzer Army hit the 106th Division, the 14th Cavalry Group and part of the 28th Division. In the south, the Seventh Army clashed with elements of the U.S. 4th, 9th Armored and 28th Divisions.

danger of such a flimsy defense, the 99th Division commander, General Walter E. Lauer, had posted two infantry battalions at the crossroads villages of Losheimergraben and Buchholz Station, on the northern edge of the gap. As an additional precaution, Bouck's platoon had been sent into the gap itself to patrol the open country and to sound a warning in case of unusual enemy activity. Bouck and his men, armed with rifles and machine guns, used as their base of operations a strong position on a high knoll near Lanzerath. They were prepared to defend themselves against anything except tanks.

On the morning of December 16, the platoon's position and the territory around it came under heavy artillery fire for about an hour. By the time the bombardment ceased, Bouck's telephone line to the nearest battalion had been severed, but he was able to get in touch with regimental headquarters by radio. He asked Major Robert L. Kriz what was going on, and Kriz replied that he was being shelled and that the whole 99th Division front had been shelled. Since Bouck had a good defensive position, Kriz ordered the platoon to stay where it was and to be on the alert for a German attack.

Moments later, Bouck and his men were dismayed to see an American tank-destroyer unit they had counted on for help suddenly pull out of Lanzerath and head for the rear. The platoon was on its own now. Bouck's runner, Private First Class William J. "Sak" Tsakanikas, remarked forlornly, "They might at least wave goodbye."

Soon afterward, the GIs spotted an enemy column approaching on a road about 100 yards below them. The Germans were walking along with their weapons slung over their shoulders, apparently convinced that all the Americans had retreated. Bouck decided to hold his fire until the main body of the column appeared. Some 200 Germans marched past. Just then a little blonde girl ran out in the road, shouted something to the Germans and hurried off. One of Bouck's men assumed that she had given away their position and began shooting. The Germans dived into a ditch on the side of the road, and a sharp skirmish ensued.

When the shooting died down, the Germans regrouped to attack the hill. They charged up from the road, wave after wave, firing their weapons as they advanced. They made it as far as a wire fence strung across an open field direct-ly in front of the American foxholes. The GIs had their guns zeroed in on the fence and stopped the attack simply by pulling their triggers. "We didn't waste many rounds," Bouck said later. "The odds were completely against them."

The Germans attacked again at midday, but again they were stopped, their dead and wounded piling high at the fence. After retreating, they waved a white flag and Bouck allowed some of them to come forward and remove their wounded comrades.

In the afternoon, the Germans attacked yet again, and again they were halted at the fence. But by late afternoon the GIs found themselves running out of ammunition. The Germans poured in fresh troops, swarmed up the knoll and finally overran the position. Bouck and his runner, Sak, were hit by rounds from a German's burp gun. Sak's face burst open, and Bouck, hit in the calf, could feel hot blood running down his leg.

A German called, "Who is the commandant? Who is the commandant?" Bouck shouted that he was in charge, and the German asked him what he and his men intended to do now. Bouck could do nothing but stand by and watch as his men were taken prisoner.

A German aid man bound up Sak's hideous wound with paper bandages and helped Bouck carry Sak through the dusk to Lanzerath. When they reached the village, the Germans led them into a dimly lighted café. Sak was deposited on a bench, barely alive. (Miraculously, he would survive the War.) Bouck slumped down on a bench. Much later, he noticed a cuckoo clock on the wall; it was nearly midnight. Remembering that the morrow, December 17, was his birthday, he said to himself, "If I can just make it until the clock hits twelve, I'll be twenty-one years old."

Bouck and his men had no way of knowing it, but their day's bloody work had blocked one of the roads earmarked for the main effort of the German drive. They had put a serious crimp in the entire offensive.

Hitler had entrusted the main attack to the Sixth Panzer Army, headed by a burly Nazi veteran, SS General Josef "Sepp" Dietrich. Dietrich had started his military career as a tank soldier in World War I. Later, he served as Hitler's bodyguard and then as commander of the Führer's personal protective force, the 1st SS Liebstandarte Adolf Hitler Regiment, which was eventually expanded to a panzer division.

Dietrich was a brave and determined soldier of limited military capacity. Nevertheless, thanks to his party loyalty and friendship with Hitler, he rose quickly in the Army. In 1942 he commanded the 1st SS Panzer Division on the Russian front, and was promoted to corps commander in 1943. To make up for Dietrich's lack of staff training, his superiors, Field Marshals von Rundstedt and Model, assigned a brilliant tactician, Brigadier General Fritz Kraemer, as chief of staff to the Sixth Panzer Army.

Dietrich's army was made up of nine divisions, but his hopes—and Hitler's—lay primarily with two of these units: his own original 1st SS Panzer Division and the 12th SS Panzer Hitler Youth Division. These elite units shared a reputation for ferocity in battle—and also for disregarding the commonly accepted rules of war. While fighting on the Eastern Front under Dietrich, men of the 1st SS once executed an estimated 4,000 Russian prisoners in reprisal for the killing of six captured SS men by Russian secret police. And the 12th SS had put to death 64 Canadian and British prisoners of war in Normandy after interrogating them.

To enable these armored units to start toward the Meuse River and Antwerp, three of Dietrich's infantry divisions were assigned to punch openings in the American front. These holes would give the tanks access to two crucial roads (map, page 59) running west toward the Meuse on roughly parallel courses. After breaking through the Losheim Gap, the 1st SS, under SS Oberführer Wilhelm Mohnke, would take the southerly route, a sequence of mediocre roads that began near Lanzerath and led to the Meuse bridge at Huy, some 50 miles away. To the north, the 12th SS, under Brigadier General Hugo Kraas, was to overrun U.S. positions on a long, high rise called the Elsenborn Ridge, then thrust west on a paved road. At the key village of Malmédy, the 12th would swing northwest through the town of Spa to the Meuse bridges at Amay and Engis, near Liège.

This northern breakthrough was particularly important; with control of the Elsenborn Ridge and the Malmédy road the Germans would be able to stop the American reinforcements that were bound to pour down from the north in an effort to choke off the advance. But both panzer divisions had to drive ahead quickly and on a broad front; otherwise, their far-ranging spearheads might be cut off from their supplies and isolated deep inside American territory.

The spearhead of the 1st SS Panzer Division was a task force built around the 1st SS Panzer Regiment and com-

manded by Lieut. Colonel Joachim Peiper, a handsome, hard-boiled bravo. At 29, Peiper was one of the youngest regimental commanders in the German Army. He possessed the kind of fanaticism that Hitler admired. On the Russian front, he had commanded a tank unit that came to be known as "the blowtorch battalion" because it reportedly burned down two villages with all their inhabitants. He had also demonstrated a flair for the kind of slashing attack he would be leading in the Ardennes. He had earned the Knight's Cross—one of Germany's highest decorations—by breaking through the Russian lines to a trapped German infantry division, collecting 1,500 wounded soldiers and bringing them safely back to German lines. For the Ardennes offensive, Peiper's regiment was reinforced to a strength of 5,000 men, and 42 mammoth Royal Tiger tanks (pages 54-55) were added to his battalion of Panthers and Mark IVs, bringing the total tank strength to about 120.

Peiper got his first inkling of his new assignment on December 10, when Dietrich's chief of staff, Kraemer, asked him whether a tank regiment could cover 50 miles in a single night. That night, Peiper borrowed a new Panther tank and took it for a test run along a road behind the German lines. The result confirmed what Peiper already knew—that a single tank could easily travel 50 miles on the open road in one night. But he carefully noted that a whole regiment could not match such a figure.

Peiper did not receive his formal briefing on the offensive until two days before the operation was to begin. On December 14, Oberführer Mohnke met with his regimental commanders, reviewed the plan of attack and passed out maps marked with the routes of advance. Peiper was distressed by his route. While the 12th SS Panzer Division on his northern flank had a good road, the secondary route assigned him was, he said, "not for tanks, but for bicycles." He complained bitterly—until he was told that Hitler himself had personally selected the routes.

The conference produced another piece of disturbing news. Mohnke told his regimental commanders that two trainloads of gasoline earmarked for the 1st SS Panzer Division had failed to arrive in the assembly area, and the attacking units would have to depend upon captured gasoline. According to German intelligence, the best bets were American fuel dumps located at Büllingen and south of Spa,

both of which were close to the route of Peiper's advance.

To conclude the conference, Mohnke read a directive from Hitler saying that the offensive must be "preceded by a wave of terror and fright and no human inhibitions should be shown." And the troops, Mohnke added, should be reminded that thousands of German women and children—perhaps members of their own families—had been killed by Allied bombing raids on German cities.

On the day of the great attack, Peiper's tanks stood poised for their lightning thrust. But they could not budge. The 12th Volksgrenadier Division, which was supposed to break through the American defenses in the early morning, was caught in a massive traffic jam on the narrow roads leading into the Losheim Gap. Peiper hurried forward to see what was holding up the Volksgrenadiers and found the road through Losheim backed up for miles with tanks, half-tracks, horse-drawn artillery and cursing drivers. The ultimate cause of the delay was a missing bridge over the railroad tracks northwest of the village. The bridge had been demolished by the Germans in their retreat through the Ardennes in September, but the planners had neglected to take that fact into account.

Impatient and disgusted, Peiper ordered his tanks "to push through rapidly and run down anything in the road ruthlessly." Plunging into the melee himself to unsnarl the traffic, he discovered a detour around the wrecked bridge and finally reached Losheim by 7:30 that night. There, he picked up a message from headquarters, informing him that another railroad overpass up ahead was out, and instructing him to detour westward through the village of Lanzerath. This would bring him into the attack zone of the German 3rd Parachute Division and near the point where an entire regiment of that unit had been held up all day by Lieutenant Bouck and his platoon.

Turning to the west, Peiper's tanks ran into a German minefield, but he ordered them to plow right through the mines. Five tanks and five other vehicles were lost in the process, but Peiper finally had his column moving.

It was after midnight when Peiper pulled into Lanzerath. He strode into the dimly lighted café where Bouck (now turned 21) was waiting with Sak and the other wounded men. After summoning the commander of the parachute regiment,

THE ROYAL TIGER: GERMANY'S TRAVELING FORTRESS

The Royal Tiger tank, with a complement of five men, was 34 feet long and 12 feet wide and weighed 68 tons, making it the heaviest tank used by any nation in World War II. The turret alone, protected by steel armor more than seven inches thick and mounting a 17-foot-long 88mm cannon, weighed 20 tons. Driven by a 700-horsepower engine, the Royal Tiger could reach a top speed of 26 miles per hour.

In June 1944, twelve huge German tanks knocked out a British armored brigade in Normandy, destroying 25 lesser tanks, 14 half-tracks and 14 Bren gun carriers in less than 10 minutes' time. For the Allies on the Western Front, it was an ominous demonstration of the power of Germany's super-tank—the Tiger. Six months later, GIs in the Ardennes faced no fewer than 250 of the monster tanks, including 45 new Royal Tigers, which had even greater firepower

and thicker armor plate, slanted to deflect shells, than its predecessor.

The Royal Tiger boasted the most powerful cannon of any tank in the Ardennes. The 22-pound shells fired from the long-barreled, high-velocity 88mm gun could knock out a thinner-skinned Sherman—the principal U.S. tank in the battle—from more than half a mile away.

By contrast, the Royal Tiger's frontal armor was six inches thick and virtually im-

The photographs above sum up the unbalanced odds in any shoot-out between a Royal Tiger tank and a U.S. Sherman tank. The slanted, heavily armored front of the Royal Tiger (top) carries scuff marks where a Sherman's 75mm shells have been deflected. The armor of the Sherman underneath, only one and a half inches thick on the vertical flanks, has been repeatedly punctured by a Tiger's more powerful cannon.

pervious to shells from any American tank, even at close range. One tank sergeant reported scoring 14 direct hits with his Sherman's cannon—without causing damage. Besides its cannon, the Royal Tiger was armed with two machine guns: one up front, the other mounted on the turret.

Because of its heavy armament and thick armor, the Royal Tiger was exactly twice as heavy as the 34-ton Sherman and was six or seven miles per hour slower. The usual

American tactic against a Royal Tiger was for several Shermans to outflank their lumbering foe and try to knock it out from the rear, where its armor was only two inches thick. But even when the tactic worked, it often cost at least one Sherman.

In fact, the Royal Tiger was not as clumsy as it seemed—thanks to several innovations in design. One was its extra-wide tracks, which made for superior traction on boggy terrain. Another, a unique drive sys-

tem, enabled the tank to turn quickly by reversing the direction of one track while keeping the other track pulling forward.

The Royal Tiger's power and size gave it yet another advantage: the Americans feared it. Some Sherman crews avoided taking on Tigers, calling such an engagement "suicidal." And at least one commander refused to order his Shermans to meet the advancing Tigers for fear that he would be disobeyed.

Peiper spread out a map on the bar but, as Bouck later recalled, the map kept slipping off; so Peiper finally nailed it to the wall with a pair of bayonets and studied it by the light of a lantern.

When the paratroop commander arrived, he turned out to be a transferred Luftwaffe colonel who knew little about infantry tactics. Under hard questioning by Peiper, the colonel admitted that his troops had not been able to achieve a breakthrough because, as he put it, "the woods up the way were full of Americans." Peiper stormed out of the café and commandeered a battalion of the paratroop infantry. At about 4 a.m. on December 17, he set out to attack Buchholz Station, the next village along the road. The assault proved to be a lark. Peiper's tanks, with the paratroopers draped aboard them, went roaring right into Buchholz Station without firing a shot.

Beyond Buchholz Station, the road was jammed with fleeing American vehicles: trucks filled with soldiers, prime movers dragging artillery pieces, ammunition carriers and kitchen trucks. Peiper's panzers simply hitched onto the tail of the retreating column and rode into the next village, Honsfeld, catching the Americans there by surprise. A GI in one house along the way heard clanking sounds in the street. He opened the door, saw a gigantic Tiger tank rumbling past, and slammed the door in a hurry. "My God!" he exclaimed. "They're German!"

In the onslaught that followed, many Americans of the 99th Division were captured or killed—and Hitler's directive to show "no human inhibitions" was given its first expression. In one house, 22 Americans were surrounded by Peiper's troops. A German 88mm gun was methodically pulverizing the building when a white flag appeared in the window. At this, the firing subsided, and a dozen Americans walked outside to surrender. As soon as they had emerged, they were shot down.

Elsewhere in Honsfeld, Peiper's troops rounded up about 200 prisoners. As these men were herded toward the rear, a German tank opened fire on them. When the shooting died down, 19 Americans were dead in the Honsfeld area.

Although Peiper's tanks had covered only a little more than 20 miles, they had burned up a lot of precious gasoline idling their engines while waiting for a breakthrough. Peiper therefore decided that, instead of continuing on his assigned route toward Stavelot, he would detour into Büllingen—on the 12th SS Panzer Division's route—to refuel his tanks in the American supply dump there.

On the way into Büllingen, Peiper's tanks came upon half a dozen American prisoners. An SS sergeant ordered his men to shoot the Americans, and the prisoners were immediately mowed down by machine-gun, rifle and pistol fire. Then the panzers roared onto a small landing field used by American artillery-observation planes and helped themselves to some 50,000 gallons of fuel, forcing 50 American prisoners to do the fueling.

In Büllingen, the Germans continued slaughtering prisoners. About 30 Americans were lined up and shot. Another group of about a dozen, marching to the rear with their hands over their heads, were fired on by machine pistols and rifles. An SS company commander beckoned to 10 American prisoners, then shot them down as they obediently approached his vehicle.

A civilian, too, fell victim. Some SS troops entered a house and asked a woman whether any Americans were hiding there. When she said no, one man put a rifle to her forehead and pulled the trigger. So far, Peiper's rampaging men had murdered at least 69 prisoners of war and the one woman. But the worst was yet to come.

To clear the road to Büllingen for the 12th SS Panzer Division, Peiper quickly pulled his troops out of the town and back onto his southern route. By midday, they were approaching the crossroads hamlet of Baugnez, two and a half miles south of Malmédy. Baugnez was not much to look at—it consisted of a café and a few farmhouses—but it commanded a critical road junction.

The roads were now jammed with American vehicles traveling in all directions. From the smashed front line came trucks, jeeps and staff cars heading westward, fleeing the onrushing Germans. At the same time, combat units with infantry and tanks were swimming against the tide, struggling southward and eastward to get to the front.

One of those front-bound units was Battery B of the 285th Field Artillery Observation Battalion, a unit that was making its way from Hürtgen Forest in the north to the town of Vielsalm, five miles to the south of Peiper's route. Trucks carrying the 140 men of Battery B rolled into Baugnez at 1 p.m., just as Peiper's advance guard reached the crossroads.

Peiper's column opened fire on Battery B with cannon and machine guns. Panicky GIs leaped from their trucks. Most of them scrambled for cover in a ditch, and the rest made a dash for a nearby patch of woods. The men in the ditch, hopelessly outnumbered and outgunned, were quickly surrounded. They crawled out with their hands in the air.

In all, about 120 men were rounded up and relieved of their carbines and rifles. They were roughly searched by a throng of high-spirited SS troopers, who helped themselves to the Americans' watches, wallets, warm gloves and cigarettes. While the GIs were being searched, a tank crewman jovially said in formal English, "First SS Panzer Division welcomes you to Belgium, gentlemen." But the Americans were not amused. They noted uneasily that the Germans' caps were lettered with the dread SS insignia and that some were decorated with a death's head.

The prisoners were lined up and prodded into a pasture near the crossroads. They stood there in ranks in the cold and mud with their hands raised in surrender while the German officers discussed their fate.

Soon some tanks and half-tracks moved up and parked opposite the field. And then the Germans opened fire on the prisoners with machine guns, machine pistols and other weapons. The Americans crumpled to the ground, the majority of them dead or wounded, a few of them unscathed but feigning death. When the firing died down, SS officers and men walked among the prostrate forms and pumped bullets into GIs who showed signs of life, or crushed their skulls with rifle butts. One soldier expertly tested each GI first by kicking him in the groin. If a victim reacted, he was shot in the head.

Sergeant Kenneth F. Ahrens was lying on the ground with a bullet in his back. "I could hear them walking down amongst the boys that were lying there," he later reported. "Naturally there was a lot of moaning and groaning, and some of the boys weren't dead yet.

"You would hear a stray shot here and a stray shot there; they were walking around making sure there was nobody left. Each time they would hear somebody moan, they would shoot him; and there was one particular time when I could feel a footstep right alongside of me, where one of the boys laid across the back of me, or this side of me, and

they shot him. But why he didn't shoot me I don't know. . . . Every once in a while a tank or a half-track would roll by and turn their guns on us, just for a good time. I mean they were laughing, they were having a good time."

Ahrens lay still all through the killings. When the shooting stopped he heard a voice whisper, "Let's go." He got up and ran across the field with two other wounded men. A machine gun and some small arms opened up, but the Americans made it safely into a patch of woods. No one pursued them. They walked about five miles until they arrived at a road, where they waited until an American captain happened by in a jeep. He took them to the American lines. Other survivors staggered into the outposts of the 291st Engineer Combat Battalion near Malmédy and were rushed to aid stations.

Accounts of the grisly episode soon led to an on-the-spot investigation. The commanding officer of the 291st, Lieut. Colonel David E. Pergrin, sent a shocking report to higher headquarters: 86 American soldiers had been killed in cold blood by the SS troops while being held as prisoners of war.

The incident quickly came to be called the Malmédy Massacre. News of the killing spread rapidly through the frontline units; it had an electrifying effect. American resolve stiffened. Some units vowed that they would take no prisoners in SS uniform.

The trail of death Peiper's men left behind at Honsfeld, Büllingen and Baugnez was a substantial contribution to the wave of terror called for by Hitler. And still more terror and confusion were to be spread by the paratroopers of Colonel von der Heydte and the commandos of Lieut. Colonel Skorzeny's Panzer Brigade 150.

Skorzeny's special troops, assigned to seize three bridges over the Meuse and to disrupt the American rear areas, were ready and eager to go on the morning of December 16. Some of the brigade's 2,000 men were dressed in American uniforms. As a further disguise, their 70 tanks included some captured American Shermans, plus some German tanks that had been crudely disguised with sheet metal in order to resemble Shermans. The brigade was to assume the role of an American unit fleeing toward the rear; plans called for it to race ahead to the Meuse River during the night of December 17, seize the bridges intact and occupy them until the arrival of leading units of the two SS panzer divisions.

But Panzer Brigade 150 was bedeviled from the very start. Like Peiper, Skorzeny went forward to Losheim on the morning of the 16th and found the road to be hopelessly jammed with vehicles, horses and troops. Skorzeny coolly decided to take a nap. When he awakened that evening, Peiper had moved on, but the Germans still had not been able to achieve a breakthrough. Skorzeny, realizing that a quick dash to the Meuse was simply not in the cards, went back to sleep. He awakened again in time to attend a war council and discuss the situation with General Dietrich. On Skorzeny's recommendation, his mission to capture the bridges was canceled, and his brigade was assigned to support the 1st SS Panzer Division.

Meanwhile, Skorzeny's commando teams were succeeding beyond his wildest hopes. Trained in the techniques of infiltration and sabotage, some 150 Germans who spoke English had set out in 30 captured American jeeps wearing American uniforms and carrying false identification papers. Although only nine commando teams managed to infiltrate Allied lines, they had a devastating psychological impact. One four-man team switched road signs at a crossroads, sending an entire American regiment rushing in the wrong direction. Another unit blocked off key roads with white tape—the GIs' standard signal warning of minefields ahead. Yet another told an American officer such a lurid tale of German successes that he withdrew his unit from the town it was occupying.

Some units were captured. One team made it all the way to the Meuse before being caught. A second group, seized by GIs near Liège, told the most outrageous cock-and-bull story of the entire operation. They said that Skorzeny and a special commando team were going to penetrate all the way to Paris; they would rendezvous at the famous Café de la Paix, head for Supreme Allied Headquarters at Versailles and assassinate General Eisenhower.

The Americans accepted the whole fantastic yarn. A cordon of troops set up an ambush around the Café de la Paix, a curfew was imposed in Paris and MPs stopped and interrogated soldiers and civilians in the streets. General Eisenhower became a virtual prisoner in his Versailles headquarters, surrounded by tripled guards, machine guns and barbed wire. Eisenhower suffered through a few days of this captivity; then he stormed out of his office and announced angrily, "Hell's fire, I'm going out for a walk. If anyone wants to

Almost a full month after the massacre of American soldiers by Joachim Peiper's SS troopers near Malmédy on December 17, a U.S. Graves Registration team performs the grim task of locating and identifying the victims. The pall of snow had preserved the bodies until Graves Registration could do its work.

shoot me, he can go right ahead. I've got to get out."

Unknown to the Supreme Commander, his security men were using an Eisenhower look-alike, Lieut. Colonel Baldwin B. Smith, as a decoy. Every day, Smith was driven in the general's command car between Ike's house and the headquarters in Versailles, saluting, flashing a simulacrum of the famous Eisenhower grin.

In the meantime, Skorzeny's phony Americans wandered about the Ardennes, spreading rumors among U.S. troops. No one could be sure whether a passing GI was friend or foe. Nervous MPs halted everyone, regardless of rank, and asked questions that presumably only a genuine American could answer: the name of Mickey Mouse's girlfriend (Minnie), the hometown of Li'l Abner (Dogpatch), the identity of "Dem Bums" (the Brooklyn Dodgers). A number of bona fide Americans came up with unsatisfactory replies. A U.S. brigadier general who said that the Chicago Cubs were in the American League was held prisoner for five hours by soldiers who had been told to look out for a "Kraut posing as a one-star general." An American captain, caught wearing snappy German boots that he vainly explained were souvenirs, spent a week in detention.

General Bradley was repeatedly halted in his staff car by zealous noncoms who seemed to delight in challenging high-ranking officers. He had a little trouble at the first stop; though he correctly identified Springfield as the capital of Illinois, his interrogator held out for Chicago. At the second stop he fielded a football question, locating the position of guard between center and tackle. At the third roadblock he was asked to identify Betty Grable's latest husband. Bradley was stumped. His GI questioner, who recognized him anyway, triumphantly informed him, "It's Harry James," and waved him on.

The paratroop operation under Colonel von der Heydte stirred further confusion, although it accomplished even less than Skorzeny's from a strictly military standpoint. Von der Heydte and his 1,000 paratroopers had been ordered to drop on a mountain called Baraque Michel, in the high, forested marshland that was known as the Hohe Venn, about seven miles north of Malmédy. The two main roads over which the Americans were expected to pour reinforcements toward Malmédy and the Elsenborn area intersected at Baraque Michel, and von der Heydte's assignment was to secure the critical road junction, denying it to the Americans until tanks of Dietrich's Sixth Panzer Army could break through to relieve him.

Von der Heydte had been given only five days to prepare his men and the transport pilots for the tricky drop; this seemed so inadequate that he called on Field Marshal Model to suggest that the operation be scrubbed. When Model asked him whether the mission stood a 10 per cent chance of succeeding, the colonel answered in the affirmative. In

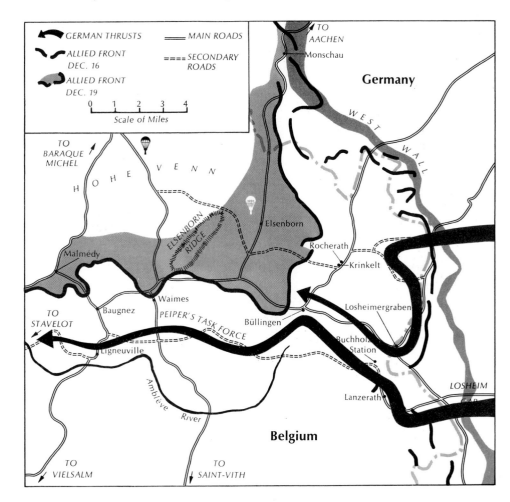

At the northern end of the Ardennes front, Peiper's SS panzer brigade quickly broke through the Losheim Gap and headed west. But the rest of the Sixth Panzer Army found its attack routes blocked by the U.S. 99th and 2nd Divisions as they withdrew toward Elsenborn Ridge. By December 19 a strong American defense zone was formed (shaded area) restricting the German breakthrough to the southern part of the sector. Two German airdrops—a small paratroop landing (red parachute) and a phony drop of 300 dummies (white parachute)—created confusion briefly in the American rear areas.

that case, said Model, the mission had to be attempted, since the chances for the whole offensive were no better than 10 per cent.

So von der Heydte dutifully proceeded to assemble his paratroopers on the night of December 15. But the trucks that were supposed to take them to the airports failed to arrive—they had run out of gasoline. The operation had to be postponed until the early morning of December 17. When the planes finally took off, they ran into strong head winds and heavy American antiaircraft fire en route to their drop zones, and the formation was widely scattered. One group of about 200 paratroopers landed far behind the German lines, near Bonn. Others, blown off course, came down in Holland. Ironically, the most successful airdrop was a fake: about 300 dummies dressed as paratroopers came to earth near Elsenborn Ridge. Some American units considered the phony drop a decoy for a real drop nearby and wasted a lot of time looking for nonexistent Germans.

Von der Heydte himself came down where he was sup-

posed to. But nearly three hours later, he had managed to assemble only 150 of his men. With such a small force, he realized that he had no hope of holding the road junction. He decided to hide near the junction and wait for the arrival of the panzer units. It was a long wait. Day after day, von der Heydte watched in frustration as units of three American divisions rolled past him on the very roads he was supposed to have cut.

For five days the panzers failed to appear. At last von der Heydte abandoned the vigil. He ordered his men to split into groups of three and make their way back to the German lines. He set out with his executive officer and a runner, sleeping in the forest undergrowth during the day and hiking by night toward Monschau at the northern end of the Ardennes front. The Sixth Panzer Army was supposed to have captured the town on the first day of the offensive, but, unknown to von der Heydte, it was still in American hands. After traveling for two days, von der Heydte and his party arrived at the outskirts of Monschau. Too exhausted to continue, von der Heydte sent his two companions on ahead while he stumbled into a house in Monschau and surrendered.

Von der Heydte's mission—the last German airborne operation of the War—had failed. But it had added substantially to the consternation behind American lines. Wild rumors spread. It was said that thousands of paratroopers had landed in Belgium and France, and that they were out to kidnap not only Eisenhower but also Bradley, Montgomery, and maybe even Prime Minister Churchill.

The most important battle on the northern Ardennes front developed rapidly near the German border, around Elsenborn Ridge. Like every other major battle in the Ardennes, the fight for the Elsenborn area was a struggle for road junctions. The ridge dominated two roads that led into the town of Büllingen, feeding the northern route to the Meuse via Malmédy. Lieut. Colonel Peiper's panzers had detoured into this area and then had withdrawn after scavenging fuel at an American dump; now General Dietrich's Sixth Panzer Army had to gain control of the feeder roads in order to launch the powerful 12th SS Panzer Division westward.

The principal feeder route ran through the border village of Losheimergraben and swung northwest to Büllingen. To

Commando Otto Skorzeny, towering over his patron, Adolf Hitler, was given only six weeks by the Führer to prepare his commandos for their disruptive behind-the-lines forays in the guise of American soldiers. But Skorzeny had executed equally urgent and unorthodox schemes before; in his greatest coup, he had rescued the ousted dictator Mussolini from a mountaintop lodge 75 miles northwest of Rome, where he was being held prisoner in 1943 by the Italian successor government. When Hitler informed Skorzeny of the commando mission, he said, "I know the time given you is very short, but I count on you to do the impossible."

THE FATE OF A GERMAN COMMANDO TEAM

A captured commando doffs his American disguise—to reveal a German uniform.

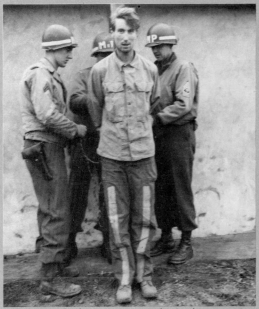

MPs tie Manfred Pernass to a stake for his execution.

With blindfolds in place and targets pinned onto their chests, the commandos wait for the fatal volley. Billing died shouting, "Heil Hitler!"

On December 18, 1944, three men, dressed in GI clothes and driving a U.S. jeep, were stopped at an American roadblock. When they could not say the password, GIs investigated and discovered that they were Officer Cadet Günther Billing, Corporal Wilhelm Schmidt and Private First Class Manfred Pernass—one of the nine teams sent out by Lieut. Colonel Otto Skorzeny (*opposite*) to spread confusion in the American rear areas.

The price of their daring was a sentence to be executed as spies. But they turned their capture into a coup of sorts by spreading alarm through the American high command with an invented tale of a plot to assassinate General Eisenhower.

Before their executions, the commandos were granted a last request—to hear German nurses in a nearby cell sing Christmas carols. The next day they went before a firing squad.

open this road for the tanks, Dietrich had assigned the task of capturing Losheimergraben to the 12th Volksgrenadier Division, considered the best infantry unit in his army. The second road ran through two adjacent villages, Krinkelt and Rocherath, and then curved southwest to Büllingen. To prevent American artillery on Elsenborn from interdicting the main Malmédy road, Dietrich had ordered the 277th Volksgrenadier Division to seize the twin villages and over-run the ridge. The 12th SS Panzer Division, commanded by General Kraas, was to wait behind the front until the infantry had opened both roads.

Dietrich anticipated no serious trouble with the American division in this area, the 99th; its troops were known to be inexperienced, and they were stretched thin, holding a line long enough for four or five divisions. But Dietrich's low estimate of their fighting was ill-founded. And his intelligence section had made an even more critical error: it had informed him that the veteran U.S. 2nd Division was resting far to the rear; in fact, most of it was attacking into Germany just to the north of the Sixth Panzer Army's planned thrusts around Elsenborn Ridge.

Dietrich turned loose his two Volksgrenadier divisions on schedule on the morning of December 16, and almost at once the 99th Division began causing trouble. German infantrymen of the 277th Division, advancing through the fog near Losheimergraben, surprised a unit of Americans while the men were waiting for breakfast in a chow line. Before the Germans could capitalize on the situation, the GIs dropped their mess kits and let loose a hail of small-arms fire. The fight went on all morning. At midday, the Germans backed off, leaving about 75 dead behind, more than twice the number of American casualties.

In front of Losheimergraben, the Germans ran into mines and barbed wire as they attacked through a heavily wooded area. Emerging from the forest around noon, they drove the Americans back about a quarter of a mile before they were finally halted by machine-gun and mortar fire. Both sides took heavy losses in a series of close-quarter skirmishes, but here too the men of the 99th fought with unexpected determination. A sergeant whose squad had been wiped out grabbed a Browning automatic rifle from a dying buddy and charged into the advancing Germans, firing as he went.

He got within 10 feet of the German column before he ran out of ammunition and was cut down.

By early afternoon the German infantry had made so little headway that Dietrich ordered some tank units into action to help out. But several of the panzers ran afoul of American antitank guns that the Volksgrenadiers had been unable to clear out. One American antitank gunner stood his ground against a huge Tiger tank as it roared down the road toward Losheimergraben. His first shot knocked off a tread, halting the tank. The gunner flung open the breech, blew the smoke from the barrel, reloaded and fired again. The Tiger burst into flames as the shell hit a thin spot in its armor. The crewmen who clambered out of the crippled tank were picked off by American rifle fire.

Reports of heavy losses prompted Dietrich to order more tanks into the battle as the day wore on. Meanwhile, in the Krinkelt-Rocherath area, some six miles to the north, the Germans attacked a second regiment of the 99th Division. They overran one company and reached a battalion command post. But then a curtain of American mortar fire drove them back. German infantry attacking another battalion ran into withering machine-gun and mortar fire as they crossed an open field. The Germans poured in reserve troops and charged the position. But the Americans counterattacked and drove the Germans back to within 400 yards of their starting point.

By nightfall, all the tanks of the 12th SS Panzer Division had been committed to the battle, and the Americans were in a precarious position. The two regiments of the 99th Division had taken a battering; they were barely holding on at Losheimergraben, and were in grave danger at Krinkelt-Rocherath. Nevertheless, the raw GIs of the 99th had put on a strong show: their commander, General Lauer, reported to V Corps headquarters at midnight that the 99th was holding not far from its original line and that, for the moment at least, the situation was in hand.

Lauer's report did not reassure the V Corps commander, General Gerow. Gerow was worried. His superior, General Hodges, had not yet called off the attack of the 2nd Division, and two of its regiments were still inching their way forward into Germany. Gerow knew that if the 2nd Division had to retreat to the Elsenborn area its route would be the Krinkelt-Rocherath road, and he feared that the road would

In a field in the northern Ardennes, curious GIs survey the wreckage of a Junkers-52 transport and its dead passengers—men from Colonel Friedrich von der Heydte's special paratroop unit. The plane, shot down by American antiaircraft fire, was one of a squadron of 112 battle-worn Ju-52s and Ju-88s ferrying the men into battle in the blustery early morning hours of December 17. The pilots were as green as the troops they bore; few had made a normal airdrop—let alone one at night in gale-force winds. Only 35 planes got to the appointed drop zone in the Hohe Venn region, and some 300 paratroopers who landed there achieved little more than to stir up alarm among the Americans.

be cut by German attacks at any moment. The two villages had to be held until the scattered units of the 2nd and 99th Divisions funneled back to the strong defensive positions atop Elsenborn Ridge.

Lacking sufficient authority to order a withdrawal himself, Gerow did what he could to bolster the beleaguered units of the 99th Division screening the twin villages on the east and southeast. He called out the reserve regiment of the 2nd Division, the 23rd, which was standing by in the town of Elsenborn, in front of Elsenborn Ridge. He sent one battalion to Losheimergraben and another to the Rocherath area. By nightfall of the 16th, the seasoned troops of the 23rd Regiment were digging in at critical points behind the battered lines of the 99th Division.

By early morning on December 17, General Hodges realized that Gerow's front was in serious trouble. He also realized that the two attacking regiments of the 2nd Division were in danger of being trapped, and that Peiper's breakthrough on the southern flank of the 99th Division threatened to cut off both divisions from the rear. Hodges therefore made two important decisions. He gave Gerow permission to defend his corps as he saw fit. And he sent out an urgent message asking for help from the veteran 1st Infantry Division, whose units were resting behind Aachen, with some of the men on leave as far away as Paris.

At 7:30 a.m. on December 17, Gerow flashed the order for withdrawal to the 2nd Division commander, Major General Walter M. Robertson. Robertson had anticipated the order and had spent time the previous day mapping out a detailed plan for a daylight withdrawal under enemy fire.

The plan involved a complicated tactic known to military men as "skinning the cat." The attacking 2nd Division units would be pulled back through their rear battalions, which would cover their withdrawal. The movement would then be repeated, with the rear battalions—now in front—falling back through the former front units, until the entire force was safely back in the Krinkelt-Rocherath area, seven and a half miles to the south. Then, with the veterans of the 2nd Division holding off the Germans, all the men of the 99th could pull back through the 2nd Division lines to form a firm line of defense on Elsenborn Ridge. There they would later be joined by the 2nd Division.

The maneuver was fraught with peril. In the fog and snow of the Ardennes winter, frontline units could easily be mistaken for the enemy and mowed down by their own rear units as they withdrew. If closely pursued by Germans, the withdrawing units could not be covered safely with fire from the rear units. And the entire chain of command was likely to collapse if units became intermingled.

Well aware of all the pitfalls, Robertson personally super-

vised the 2nd Division withdrawal, orchestrating the redeployment of units and frequently directing traffic. On the morning of the 17th, he pulled the 9th Regiment back through the 38th and started it down the road to Rocherath. As units of the 9th arrived there, he placed some of them at strategic points to hold open the northern approaches to Rocherath for the 38th Regiment, which came down the road later in the day. Other 9th Regiment units took up position at Krinkelt junction, where a forest road branched off the main road and led to Elsenborn Ridge.

As these moves were taking place, new threats seemed to be developing. In the early morning hours of the 17th, German infantry and tanks renewed their desperate assaults on the two 99th Division regiments and the bolstering units of the 2nd Division's reserve regiment. To the south, fresh assaults by the 12th Volksgrenadiers drove one battalion of the 99th from Losheimergraben, nearly destroying the unit. Another battalion had to retreat so hastily toward Elsenborn Ridge that it left many wounded men behind.

At about the same time, a reconnoitering tank company from Peiper's spearhead threatened the unguarded 2nd Division headquarters at the village of Wirtzfeld. When the German panzers appeared on the horizon only 600 yards from his command post, General Robertson announced grimly, "We are going to hold this CP." His headquarters staff—cooks, clerks and orderlies—proceeded to knock out two tanks and an armored car in the first five minutes of battle. The cooks and clerks held on until the only remaining infantry in the area, an uncommitted battalion of the 23rd Regiment, rushed south and dug in on a ridge between Büllingen and their divisional CP.

Peiper's probe was driven off. But by then the 277th Volksgrenadiers, strongly reinforced by 12th SS Panzer tanks and troops, had renewed the attack on the 99th Division positions east of Krinkelt-Rocherath. The exhausted Americans were pushed back through the thin second line of defense, which was manned by a battalion of the 23rd Regiment. While the men of the 23rd held their positions, one of their company commanders, Captain Charles MacDonald, spotted some 99th Division troops coming toward him on their retreat toward Elsenborn Ridge.

"A ragged column of troops appeared over the wooded ridge," Captain MacDonald later recalled. "There were not over two hundred men, the remnants of the nine hundred who had fought gallantly to our front since they were hit by the German attack the preceding day. Another group the size of a platoon withdrew along the highway, donating the few hand grenades and clips of ammunition which they possessed to my 1st Platoon."

Then German infantrymen stormed MacDonald's line, exchanging volley after volley with his GIs. "Germans fell left and right," MacDonald remembered. "The few rounds of artillery we did succeed in bringing down caught the attackers in the draw to our front, and we could hear their screams of pain when the small arms fire would slacken. But still they came!

"Seven times they came, and seven times they were greeted by a hail of small arms fire and hand grenades that sent them reeling down the hill, leaving behind a growing pile of dead and wounded."

Eventually the Germans brought up five Tiger tanks and drove MacDonald's company back under point-blank cannon fire. But the 2nd Division men gave ground grudgingly. Private First Class Richard E. Cowan covered the company's withdrawal with its only remaining machine gun. After the foxholes around him were all overrun, Cowan cut down wave after wave of enemy troops. An 88mm shell from a Tiger tank exploded so close that Cowan was knocked from his weapon, but he jumped back and resumed firing, and cut down about 40 German infantrymen advancing with the tanks. Cowan kept firing until he ran out of ammunition. Then he left the gun and trudged toward Krinkelt.

The gallantry of Cowan and others slowed the German onslaught long enough to permit the 2nd Division's 9th and 38th Regiments to withdraw safely to the twin villages. The 400 survivors of MacDonald's battalion made it back to Krinkelt and joined forces with the other 2nd Division troops in the area. But by the evening of the 17th, German armored units began jabbing holes in the thinly held American lines around the twin villages. Throughout the night, the battle for Krinkelt raged from hedgerow to hedgerow and from house to house. Repeatedly the Germans broke through, only to be driven back by fierce counterattacks.

In adjacent Rocherath the same sort of fighting raged all night long, while troops and vehicles of the retreating 99th Division streamed through on their way to Elsenborn Ridge.

At one point, the units were so intermixed that a 2nd Division battalion commander had men from 16 different companies fighting under him. Though the tide of battle surged back and forth, the Americans were still in possession of both Rocherath and Krinkelt throughout the night.

Just before daybreak, the Germans renewed their assaults. Tanks of the 12th SS Panzer Division burst into Rocherath and pushed up to a regimental command post. They were hurled back by artillery fire from Elsenborn Ridge, by bazooka fire and antitank mines, and sometimes by cans of gasoline poured on the tanks and set afire. On the outskirts of the village, a 2nd Division lieutenant named Stephen P. Truppner called in artillery fire on his own position after more than half his company had been wiped out. He radioed that the "artillery is coming in fine," then signed off. When the 12 surviving men of his company finally straggled out, Truppner was not among them.

Everyone took part in the defense. A cook's helper in the 38th Regiment grabbed a bazooka and knocked out two panzers, blocking the tanks advancing behind them. Even crippled U.S. tanks played a key role: Two Shermans, immobilized in a lane in Rocherath, picked off five huge Tigers as they rumbled by, exposing their vulnerable rear armor.

All day long, men of the 99th continued to trickle back through the 2nd Division lines from the north, east and south. General Lauer compared his disrupted 99th to "a giant ant heap that has been kicked over, with the ants scurrying around in frantic effort to repair the damage done." Lauer described the turmoil: "Aid stations overflowing, wounded men being evacuated by jeep, truck, ambulance, anything that could roll, walking wounded, prisoners going back under guard, trucks rolling up to the front with ammunition and supplies and firing at the same time at low-flying airplanes. Vehicles off the road, mired in mud or slush or damaged by gun fire only to be manhandled off the traffic lane to open the road; signal men trying to string wire to elements cut off or to repair lines which were being shot out as fast as they were put in."

To add further to this confusion, Lauer's troops and the men of the 2nd Division had become so thoroughly entangled that the 99th temporarily ceased to exist as an integral force, and General Gerow appointed General Robertson to act as the temporary commander of both divisions.

But by nightfall on December 18th, the last organized units of the 99th Division had made their way back through the 2nd Division's lines, completing the two outfits' complex withdrawal. During the three-day operation, their battered lines had repeatedly thrown back attacks by three divisions of the Sixth Panzer Army. Not a single one of the 12th SS panzers had broken through to the Malmédy road.

Now, under orders from his superiors, General Dietrich abandoned the armored attack on the twin villages. On the night of December 18, he swung the 12th SS Panzer around for an attempt to reach the Malmédy road from the south. This tactic also failed. While traveling south on the muddy secondary roads, many heavy tanks bogged down. Some, in fact, sank in the goo all the way up to their turrets. In any case, the move was too late. By now, experienced soldiers of the 1st Infantry Division had arrived and had formed a solid wedge of defense that sealed off the southern approach to the Malmédy road.

The departure of the 12th SS Panzers made it relatively easy for the 2nd Division to pull back to Elsenborn Ridge. The weary GIs retreated through Krinkelt-Rocherath and reached the ridge on the night of December 19. They were solidly dug in by the morning of the 20th.

In the meantime, the American front had been further strengthened; other units of the 1st Division arrived on the southern flank, and the veteran 9th Division, which had arrived in a hurry from the vicinity of Aachen, was digging in on the northern flank. Together with the 2nd and 99th Divisions, these fresh troops formed a strong line of defense stretching wedgelike from Monschau in the north to a point near Büllingen in the south and west to Waimes. Three times on December 20, the Germans tried to break through the 99th Division, but they were driven back each time.

The failure of these assaults made it obvious to the German High Command that the battering-ram tactics of Dietrich's Sixth Panzer Army would not dislodge the Americans from Elsenborn Ridge. The German penetration into the northern Ardennes had been limited to the narrow avenue of attack opened by Peiper's spearhead unit. At a cost of 6,000 casualties, the green troops of the 99th Division and the veterans of the 2nd had dealt the Germans a critical blow. Henceforth, the Fifth Panzer Army to the south would have to carry the main weight of Hitler's offensive.

THE GERMAN JUGGERNAUT

Checking a highway sign at an Ardennes crossroads, an SS trooper riding in an amphibious vehicle confirms a route of advance for the 1st SS Panzer Division.

"DRIVE FAST AND HOLD THE REINS LOOSE"

"Goodbye, Lieutenant, see you in America," shouted a tank commander of the 1st SS Panzer Division as he set off full throttle into the Ardennes on the foggy morning of December 16, 1944. The commander's jaunty farewell captured the optimism, high spirits and reckless abandon that animated the 300,000 German attackers. The troops were delighted to be taking the offensive again after months of fighting just to hold their ground. This grand assault, they believed, would be a repeat of the 1940 blitzkrieg, unfolding in stylish obedience to an order issued to the Sixth Panzer Army: "Drive fast and hold the reins loose."

The attack achieved complete surprise. Boasted Lieut. General Hasso von Manteuffel, commander of the Fifth Panzer Army: "My storm battalions infiltrated rapidly into the American front—like raindrops." Hard on the heels of the elite infantry came hundreds of huge Tiger, Panther and Mark IV tanks, relentlessly overrunning everything that lay in their path. Top officers played frontline roles in the headlong advance. Major General Fritz Bayerlein, commander of the crack Panzer Lehr Division, boldly rode at the head of his lead column; when his staff officers argued against such a foolhardy risk, Bayerlein said, "It's not important whether I'm killed."

Field Marshal Walther Model, directing the offensive, kept a sharp lookout for slowdowns, and when a traffic jam blocked the road to Saint-Vith, the monocled commander strode out and personally unraveled the snarl.

By the end of the third day, armored columns from several German divisions had broken through the thin American defenses and were driving well into the Ardennes, recapturing towns and villages they had lost a few months before. "Resistance tended to melt whenever the tanks arrived in force," said Manteuffel. By December 19, Lieut. Colonel Joachim Peiper's combat group had covered 30 miles— more than half the distance to the Meuse River. "What glorious hours and days we are experiencing," a soldier wrote home, "always advancing and smashing everything. Victory was never so close as it is now."

Field Marshal Walther Model (center) confers with officials of the Nazi Party before launching Hitler's large-scale offensive in the Ardennes.

A heavily armed SS panzer trooper radiates the confidence and excitement that pervaded the German armies after their early victories in the Ardennes.

INFANTRYMEN OPEN THE WAY

Storming an enemy position, infantrymen of the 2nd SS Panzer Division sprint over a muddy road blocked by abandoned U.S. vehicles.

Barking orders and pointing the way, a panzer officer hurries his men past a disabled American half-track. Sizable infantry units were also included in all panzer divisions.

Soldiers attached to the 2nd SS Panzer Grenadier Regiment, screened by smoke from a burning American jeep, race forward to keep pace with their demanding timetable.

Panther tank crewmen, one of them cupping his ears to ward off the cold, ride on top for better vision during the attack.

Rumbling along a road in the Ardennes, Panther tanks take advantage of a heavy cloud cover that grounded Allied fighters.

German gunners of the 2nd SS Panzer Division keep a sharp lookout for enemy troops as their armored tank destroyer moves up in the northern Ardennes.

SOLIDIFYING THE SWIFT ADVANCE

Directing traffic, a German military policeman
sends a camouflaged supply truck forward
while an empty truck returns for reloading.

Barreling along a snowy Ardennes road in
the wake of the combat troops, a German staff
car passes signs put up by the Americans.

German engineers, charged with improving
routes, carry a raft to traverse the Our River. On
the far side is a disabled American truck.

A BONANZA OF CAPTURED EQUIPMENT

A colonel and some soldiers of the 62nd Volksgrenadier Division drive through Vielsalm, Belgium, in a captured American jeep.

Panzer troopers pause during their attack to survey a big haul of American vehicles that had been left behind by the 30th Division.

Advancing soldiers of the 2nd SS Panzer Division walk away with cans of much-needed fuel left in an abandoned American camp.

Surrendering to officers of the 1st SS Panzer Division, an American points with an upheld hand, asking if he should head to his left.

German soldiers discuss the disposition of captured American troops. One of the Germans is shouldering an antitank Panzerfaust.

Scores of American soldiers captured in the Ardennes are marched to the rear, bound for prisoner-of-war camps in Germany.

Two Germans salvage clothing and equipment from the muddy bodies of machine-gunned American soldiers. The trooper at right checks the fit of socks and boots that he has stripped from one corpse (far left).

Carrying a bundle of booty past a demolished American jeep, a German soldier moves quickly through the snow in order to catch up with his comrades ahead. They too have paused in the advance to search for spoils.

3

Eisenhower gets another star—and a bushel of oysters
Six-to-one odds against the Americans
Hot meals for GI snipers
German gunners zero in on the Stars and Stripes
Manteuffel's argument with Hitler
"No retreat. Nobody comes back."
Last-ditch stand in the Clervalis Hotel
A colonel reappears "like a ghost come to life"
General Jones's agonizing decision
A vital airdrop strangled in red tape
Disaster befalls a U.S. division

December 16, 1944, was memorable for General Eisenhower even before he learned that the Germans had attacked in the Ardennes. That day he received word from Washington that he had been promoted to five-star rank. The promotion capped a spectacular rise for Eisenhower. Between the Wars, promotions had been slow, and as late as 1936 he was a major—a rank he had held for 15 years. Over the course of the next three and a half years, he had been promoted six times. Now he was being elevated to the Army's highest rank.

Eisenhower had a light schedule that day at his headquarters at Versailles. He wrote to Prime Minister Churchill, extending best wishes for Christmas and the New Year, and answered a letter from Field Marshal Montgomery at his field headquarters in Brussels. Monty had written to say that he would like "to hop over to England" for Christmas; he also reminded Ike of a wager that they had made more than a year earlier. In October of 1943, about a month after the Allied landings in Italy, Eisenhower had bet Montgomery £5 that the war in Europe would be finished by Christmas of 1944. Montgomery now claimed that it was time for Ike to pay up. In his reply, Eisenhower conceded that Monty was likely to win the wager; but he added that Christmas was still nine days away and that he did not intend to pay until the last minute.

Later, the Supreme Commander attended the wedding of his orderly, Sergeant Michael J. "Mickey" McKeogh, and following a reception held in his quarters, he awaited the arrival of General Bradley, who was coming from his headquarters in the Luxembourg capital to talk about infantry replacements for his Twelfth Army Group. Eisenhower had planned a special treat for dinner that night with Bradley. President Roosevelt's press secretary, Stephen Early, had sent Eisenhower a bushel of fresh oysters by plane. Eisenhower was so fond of oysters that he was going to have them raw as an appetizer, in a stew for the main course and also fried for dessert.

When Bradley arrived, Eisenhower took him directly to a briefing room. During their talk, they were interrupted by a colonel from Eisenhower's intelligence section. The colonel's news was that the Germans were attacking in the Ardennes, in the sector held by General Middleton's VIII Corps. The reports were fragmentary, but they indicat-

THE BIG BREAKTHROUGH

ed that the American lines had been penetrated at several points and that a serious threat appeared to be developing in the Losheim Gap.

Bradley took the news calmly; he guessed that the Germans were merely trying to draw U.S. troops away from Patton's Third Army, which was getting ready to launch a new offensive in the Saar, far to the south of the Ardennes. But Eisenhower suspected that the attack was something more than a diversion. "I think you had better send Middleton some help," he said to Bradley.

At the time, there were only four uncommitted American divisions on the Western Front. The 82nd and 101st Airborne Divisions, which constituted the European theater reserve, were resting and refitting near Rheims after the costly *Market-Garden* operation in Holland. The 7th Armored Division was with the Ninth Army in Holland, and the 10th Armored was in reserve in Patton's zone to the south. Eisenhower suggested sending the two mobile armored divisions to the Ardennes. Bradley agreed, but noted that Patton could be expected to protest the loss of the 10th Armored on the eve of his offensive in the Saar.

Eisenhower's response was: "Tell him that Ike is running this damned war."

Bradley called Patton at his headquarters in Nancy and got the response he expected. Patton complained that the Germans were just trying to spoil his attack. But Bradley was firm, and Patton reluctantly but promptly put through the order that started the 10th Armored Division on its way to the Ardennes. Bradley's staff then relayed Ike's order to the Ninth Army Commander, Lieut. General William H. Simpson, who agreed to rush the 7th Armored south to the VIII Corps sector.

Eisenhower and Bradley then went off to dinner. To Ike's chagrin, Bradley was allergic to oysters, and the cook had to whip up a dish of scrambled eggs.

Eisenhower's decision to send Middleton help at once was a shrewd intuitive move. But its benefits were at least a day away; the two armored divisions would take that long to reach the Ardennes and have any significant effect on the obscure situation there. In the meantime, the troops caught in the German attack would have to stand firm. This was no small task. Though the American commanders did not yet realize it, the GIs were outnumbered by as much as 6 to 1 in some sectors *(map, page 87)*.

The two American divisions in the south were manning their 18-mile-long front with fewer than half of their troops in the line. But all through the first day of the attack, they fought hard and with some success against four infantry divisions of General Brandenberger's Seventh Army. At the northern edge of Brandenberger's sector, two of his infantry divisions drove a wedge through the understrength U.S. 28th Infantry Division, cutting off and infiltrating the southernmost of its three regiments. A few miles farther south, a German Volksgrenadier division got a stiff battle from a single combat command of the 9th Armored Division that had been put in the line to get some fighting experience. And below that sector, at the southern end of the German assault zone, Brandenberger's best division—the 212th Volksgrenadiers—had its hands full with a single regiment of the 4th Division.

That regiment, the 12th Infantry, numbered 3,000 men—on paper. Because the front had been so quiet, the commander of the regiment, Colonel Robert H. Chance, had sent many of his men off on pass to Luxembourg city and Paris. As a result, only five of the regiment's 12 companies were manning its outpost line—a string of picture postcard villages on the west bank of the Sûre (also known as the Sauer) River.

When German shells came whistling in on the morning of December 16, an officer sensed that the bombardment represented considerably more than the usual harassing fire. He phoned his battalion commander and said he thought that major German forces were approaching. He was interrupted in midsentence by a German-accented voice announcing triumphantly, "We are here."

The cocky Volksgrenadier who had tapped the telephone line was part of an advance detachment that had crossed the river in rubber boats before the artillery bombardment began. The remainder of the German division crossed the Sûre later in the morning, quickly overrunning most of the Americans' forward outposts and surrounding all five of the 12th Regiment's forward companies.

The veteran infantrymen of the 12th were stunned by the sudden German assault, but they showed no sign of panic. In Echternach, one company fell back to a hat factory on the edge of town and turned it into a strong point blocking the main road toward Luxembourg city. In the nearby village of Berdorf, First Lieutenant John L. Leake gathered 60 men of his company at the Parc Hotel, a three-story structure that in peacetime had catered to the area's thriving tourist trade. Leake's men were soon surrounded by strong enemy forces, but the enemy's probing attacks did not prevent the Americans from taking full advantage of the hotel's facilities. While the riflemen sniped at the Germans from hotel windows, the company cook served them hot meals prepared in the basement kitchen.

In his headquarters in the Luxembourg capital, the 4th Division commander, Major General Raymond O. Barton, was soon informed of the plight of his five frontline companies, and he radioed them a firm message: he would countenance "no retrograde movement" in the 12th Regiment sector. The garrison at Echternach acknowledged the order, but Leake and his men in Berdorf could not be raised. To contact his missing outfit, Colonel Chance got 10 tanks from an attached armored battalion and sent them as a relief force. Five tanks with riflemen on their decks drove into Berdorf and their crews, mistaking the Parc Hotel for a German strong point, began shelling it. The bombardment did not let up until one of Leake's men located an American flag and unfurled the Stars and Stripes on the hotel roof. The tanks then joined forces with Leake.

Unhappily for the Americans, however, the flag proved to be an excellent aiming point for German gunners who were positioned on the opposite bank of the Sûre River. Mortar, rocket and artillery fire rained down on the hotel, smashing the roof and upper story. But on the night of December 17, a task force of the 10th Armored Division arrived from the south, and the following morning it launched a strong counterattack into Berdorf. The newcomers linked up with Leake and a platoon of armored engineers, and together they engaged the Germans in fierce house-to-house fighting.

In the meantime, other units of the 10th Armored Division managed to battle their way through to the hat factory at Echternach. The tank commander offered to provide cover for the withdrawal of this garrison to a safer position, but Captain Paul H. Dupuis declined. General Barton had ordered them to stay put, explained Dupuis, and as far as he was concerned that order was still in effect. The tanks withdrew as darkness came.

Dupuis's infantrymen held out in the factory against increasing German pressure for four days. Then, on the 20th of December, the Germans finally succeeded in breaking through and forced the survivors to surrender. The German commander, Brigadier General Franz Sensfuss of the 212th Volksgrenadiers, came forward to accept the surrender and to have a close look at the small force that had caused his division so much trouble.

On the same day, the Germans also threw reinforcements into their attack in Berdorf. In the course of the savage fighting there, the task force of the 10th Armored Division was forced back, and the Parc Hotel came under renewed assault by enemy troops who, using demolition charges,

blew a hole in one wall of the hotel. Finally, the order came through for Leake to withdraw. He and his men clambered aboard the tanks and half-tracks and pulled back two miles under covering fire provided by the 10th Armored Division artillery.

Although the weary GIs of the 4th Division had been forced to yield ground, they had blunted the attack of the entire German Seventh Army for five days. To the north, the lone combat command of the 9th Armored Division pulled back in good order to the southwest, holding the Germans to penetrations of less than five miles. A little farther along the line, the isolated regiment of the 28th Infantry Division managed to restrain infiltrating Volksgrenadiers for nearly two days while falling back across a branch of the Sûre River; the Americans blew the bridges behind them and eventually joined forces with the combat command of the 9th Armored and 4th Infantry Division units to the southeast. Together with most of the 10th Armored Division, these units and the newly arrived 5th Infantry Division established a new line of defense stretching from the Echternach area in the east to the village of Grosbous almost 20 miles to the west.

The net result of this confused battle was a signal American success. At the cost of approximately 2,000 casualties, the GIs had established a solid line of defense blocking any enemy expansion to the south. This southern shoulder, together with the matching shoulder formed by the 99th and 2nd Divisions on Elsenborn Ridge in the north, restricted the enemy onslaught to the central portion of the Ar-

dennes. The Germans now had to funnel all their strength into a much smaller road network than they had originally planned on, and they would be much more vulnerable to blocking actions by American units in the narrow attack corridor.

While Brandenberger's army in the south was stalled and Dietrich's army in the north was making limited progress, General von Manteuffel in the center was launching what would develop into the main attack of the entire German offensive. Hitler's strategy in the Ardennes had originally called for Manteuffel's Fifth Panzer Army to play a secondary role. Attacking to the south of Dietrich's Sixth Panzer Army, Manteuffel's forces were supposed to break through the American defenses and go streaking for the Meuse. But once that river was crossed, they were to head northwest and protect the southern flank of Dietrich's army while it accomplished the offensive's major objective, the capture of Antwerp.

The success of the Fifth Panzer Army's attack was in large part a product of the tactics devised by Manteuffel himself. An imaginative panzer expert who had served with distinction in North Africa and Russia, Manteuffel had planned his

Unaware of the German counteroffensive in the Ardennes, Supreme Allied Commander Dwight D. Eisenhower (far left) signs the guest book at the palace at Versailles on December 16, 1944. The general had come to the palace chapel from his nearby headquarters to attend the wedding of his orderly, Sergeant Michael J. "Mickey" McKeogh, to WAC Pearlie Hargrave (left). After the ceremony, Eisenhower returned to his headquarters to preside at the reception. Not until that evening did he receive the first report that the Germans had counterattacked.

Lieut. General Hasso von Manteuffel, commander of the Fifth Panzer Army, joined the Ardennes offensive with a reputation as a brilliant, brave field leader. In just six years, he had risen from major to commander of an army and had become the 24th man to be awarded diamonds for his Knight's Cross with oak leaves and crossed swords.

assault with meticulous care, and he had shown considerable courage by disputing several aspects of Hitler's master plan for his army.

Most important, the general had persuaded the Führer that the infantry should attack first, rather than panzers, as Hitler had originally planned; the foot soldiers would open paths for the armor, clearing out enemy tank-destroyer units. Manteuffel then argued against Hitler's plan for the artillery to open fire at 7:30 a.m. and for the infantrymen to launch their attack at 11 a.m. "All our artillery will do at 7:30 is to wake up the Americans," Manteuffel said, "and they will have three and a half hours to organize their countermeasures before our assault comes." The general made the further point that, in the middle of December, darkness would begin to settle in by 4 o'clock in the afternoon. If the infantry attack was not launched until 11 a.m., only five hours of daylight would remain for the troops to achieve a breakthrough. He proposed instead that both the artillery bombardment and the infantry attack be launched at 5:30 a.m., adding five and a half hours to the effective time allotted for the first-day breakthrough. Hitler also agreed to this change.

Having shaped the key features of the planned offensive to his liking, Manteuffel set about organizing his attack to achieve the maximum impact and surprise. He decided to send small units forward to infiltrate enemy frontline positions before the artillery opened fire. In some areas, he dispensed entirely with artillery preparation: Special storm battalions, composed of the finest officers and men in each division, would move forward stealthily, bypass the enemy positions and penetrate deep into rear areas before the Americans had a chance to coordinate an effective reaction. Over most of the Fifth Panzer Army's 28-mile front, tanks would not go into action until dark at the end of the first day. Navigating under "artificial moonlight"—searchlights bounced off the low-hanging clouds—the tanks would push forward and exploit the infantry breakthroughs with decisive force and speed.

Manteuffel planned his dispositions to suit the terrain and to make the most effective use of the forces at his disposal: one infantry and two panzer corps—a total of four infantry and three panzer divisions, plus one panzer brigade, the Führer Begleit, Hitler's old escort battalion. He picked his best commanders to lead the two panzer corps, Lieut. General Heinrich F. von Lüttwitz and Lieut. General Walter Krüger. The more aggressive Lüttwitz was assigned a wide sector in the southern part of the army's attack zone, where the terrain beyond the rugged, stream-crossed front was relatively open and afforded the best opportunities for tanks. Krüger's corps was placed along a narrower sector in the center of Manteuffel's zone.

The infantry corps, under the command of Lieut. General Walther Lucht, was deployed at the northern end of the front, where the terrain was least suited to cross-country tank movements. The way was barred here by the heavily forested ridge known as the Schnee Eifel, but there were several natural routes around both ends of the ridge that could be readily exploited by infantry units. At the northern end of the Schnee Eifel lay the seven-mile-wide Losheim Gap, and at the southern end lay the three-mile-wide valley of the Alf River. Roads running through these broad depressions converged to the west at Saint-Vith, the road and rail center that was the first major objective of Manteuffel's attack. The general hoped to take Saint-Vith by the second day of the offensive.

Manteuffel based his timetable on the thinness of the U.S. defenses in the Fifth Panzer Army's zone of action. The newly arrived 106th Division was deployed along a 20-mile front that followed the West Wall and included the Schnee Eifel, a vulnerable salient jutting eight miles into Germany. The remainder of the front was held by two regiments of the 28th Division, which were stretched out over a distance of about 15 miles. Manteuffel had good reason to expect a clean breakthrough across the Clerf River by the end of the first day.

Manteuffel's clever planning, together with crisp execution by most of his divisions, got his army off on the right foot. In the predawn darkness of December 16, before the bombardment began, his storm battalions penetrated the American lines and advanced rapidly. "At 4 o'clock in the afternoon," Manteuffel later wrote, "the tanks advanced and pressed forward in the dark with the help of 'artificial moonlight.' By that time bridges had been built over the Our River. Crossing these about midnight, the armored divisions reached the American main position at 8 a.m.,

German armies attacking in the south and central Ardennes fared unequally during the first four days of the offensive. At the southern end, one division of the Seventh Army broke through to Wiltz, but three others were stopped by the Americans on a line (shaded area) between Echternach and Grosbous. In the center, the Fifth Panzer Army wrung out sizable gains; in the main attack, four divisions broke through and drove toward Bastogne. Farther north, a panzer division and a Volksgrenadier division launched a two-pronged assault on Houffalize.

then called for artillery support and quickly broke through."

But Manteuffel soon learned to his annoyance that the breakthroughs had not settled anything. While his vanguards pressed forward, many small bypassed American units formed pockets of resistance in what had become the German rear.

On the 16th, two regiments of the U.S. 28th Division were hit by a 45-minute bombardment and then found themselves fighting two entire German corps. The 112th Regiment, defending a six-mile-long front, held off the infantry of General Krüger's corps through the first day. But the commander of the 112th realized that his exposed positions on the far bank of the Our River could not be held much longer. He ordered his companies to disengage and work their way back to the west bank on the night of the 17th. Most of the men managed to slip across a bridge at the village of Ouren. One patrol reached another bridge and found it guarded by Germans. The men lined up in forma-

tion and, with their sergeant shouting commands in German, marched across in the darkness under the noses of the unsuspecting enemy guards.

The next morning, Krüger's tanks attacked in large numbers. They were briefly halted by deadly artillery fire and by the bombs of some U.S. fighter-bombers flying in the face of fog and rain. But then the Germans advanced steadily.

Manteuffel's main thrust hit to the south of the 112th, in the zone of the 110th Regiment. Spread over a 15-mile front along the road known to the Americans as Skyline Drive, the 110th was attacked by three German divisions of General von Lüttwitz's 47th Panzer Corps, including the formidable 2nd Panzer and Panzer Lehr Divisions.

The commander of the 110th Regiment was Colonel Hurley E. Fuller, a tough and irascible veteran of World War I. Fuller was headquartered some five miles west of the front in the Clervalis Hotel in Clervaux, a resort town that was used as a headquarters and rest area. At the start of the attack, Fuller's telephone lines were knocked out and his

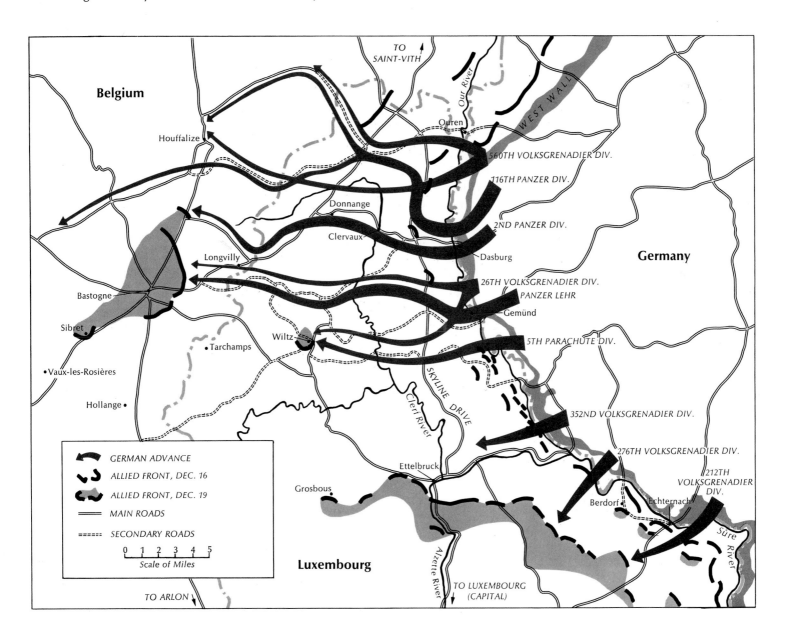

radio wavelengths jammed. He struggled to piece together rumors and isolated reports.

Gradually, Fuller learned that enemy troops were moving through his two forward battalions, obscured by the half-light and dense ground fog. Then an excited messenger ran in to announce that German infantrymen and tanks had crossed the Our River and were heading west en masse, swarming into the forest glens like ants. Fuller saw, outside in the streets, little knots of panicky townspeople asking the soldiers who rushed by what was going on. The GIs, most of them in the rest center on a pass, knew only one thing: they had to get back to their units as fast as they could. Fuller scraped together a dozen or so tanks and a force of about 200 men and prepared to defend Clervaux. But many of the men were clerks, MPs, bakers and cooks attached to headquarters.

By dawn of December 17, German units had advanced eight miles from river crossings at Dasburg and Gemünd, seizing villages and strong points along the way. Some Volksgrenadiers had already reached the outskirts of Clervaux and were firing machine guns at a château where Fuller's headquarters company was billeted. Fuller sent his tanks to relieve his besieged outposts, but they were beaten back by twice as many German panzers. In one sharp engagement, 11 Shermans ran up against 30 big Tigers. All of the Shermans were hit and set afire.

Fuller's men fought and lost skirmishes all morning long. At 11:30 a.m., the colonel put through a second desperate call to his division commander, Major General Norman D. "Dutch" Cota, headquartered in the town of Wiltz, about 10 miles to the southwest. Fuller shouted, "I need more artillery support, more tanks!"

"I'll send you a battery of self-propelled guns," Cota replied. "And that's all I can spare. I've got two other regiments screaming for help."

"And we've got 12 Tigers sitting on the high ground east of town, looking down our throats."

"Sorry, Fuller, one battery is all I can give you. Remember your orders. Hold at all costs. No retreat. Nobody comes back."

There was a moment of silence on the other end. "Do you understand, Fuller?" Cota asked.

"Yes, sir," the colonel replied. "Nobody comes back."

By 3 p.m. on December 17, the armored ring around Clervaux had almost closed. Most of Fuller's strong points had been overrun, and the panzers were heading into town from three directions. The GIs fought on gallantly, but an hour later they were giving ground faster. As afternoon turned into night, Fuller frantically phoned his company commanders, ordering them to hold back the Germans to the last man.

Suddenly a loud explosion shook the floor under his feet, followed by two more explosions and a burst of machine-gun fire that slammed into the plaster above his head. In the street below, at a range of 15 yards, a German tank was methodically pulverizing the hotel. The walls shook, the lights flickered out, the phone went dead.

Fuller decided to move out and regroup somewhere else. Quickly, he gathered up his staff and the command-post platoon, which included several wounded men, and headed through a window at the rear. With a blinded soldier hanging onto his belt, the colonel led the way up a steel ladder leaning against a steep cliff behind the hotel. At the top he flopped to the ground panting, then turned to look down at the town. Clervaux was an inferno of burning buildings. A procession of Panther tanks rumbled through the rubble-filled streets, firing their cannon point-blank at houses in which GIs were still holding out. Overhanging everything was a pall of oily smoke, pierced here and there by the white fingers of German searchlights bounced off the clouds to illuminate the attack.

One by one, the last pockets of resistance in Clervaux were eliminated. A hundred men of the headquarters company held out in the burning château. When German troops stormed through the building, they found nearly everyone dead or wounded. They met one strange sight: In a baronial hall deep in the château a lone American soldier sat playing a piano while rubble sifted down over him.

Colonel Fuller was taken prisoner as he attempted to rally stragglers near Wiltz. On hearing of his capture, a sergeant who knew him well said, "The Krauts will sure be sorry they took Hurley."

The Germans were rolling westward past Clervaux now, and General Middleton at VIII Corps headquarters flung new obstacles in their path. In the early morning of December

18, GI units built and defended roadblocks at two key junctions along the main road from Clervaux to Bastogne—less than 20 miles to the west. But the first barricade was overrun by 2 o'clock in the afternoon; the second came under fire in the early evening and fell during the night. Sweeping westward to Longvilly, the Germans overran another hastily organized defensive position near Donnange, forcing the defenders back to a perimeter being organized around Bastogne just six miles away.

Middleton had been alerted to the fall of Clervaux by a phone call from General Cota, who also warned the corps commander that elements of the 110th Regiment were holding out in other villages with no hope of stopping the Germans. Middleton reluctantly instructed Cota to pull out the shattered remnants of the regiment and move them back beyond the Clerf River.

Cota decided now to concentrate on holding his division headquarters at Wiltz, an important junction town along the southern route to Bastogne. In Fuller's absence, Cota entrusted the defense of Wiltz to Colonel Daniel B. Strickler, executive officer of the 110th Regiment. Strickler was given a makeshift task force: infantry—including clerks, drivers, mechanics and bandsmen from the division headquarters—and portions of a tank battalion and a field-artillery battalion.

On December 19 the Germans were fast closing in, and Strickler improvised a defense line around Wiltz and sent tanks out to bolster key points. But by midafternoon the situation was desperate. That evening the Germans mounted a major attack, broke through in the south and threatened to overrun the town completely. The GIs were by now numb with weariness; many units were out of ammunition, and the Germans held all of the roads leading into and out of Wiltz.

Strickler called the unit commanders together and told them to fight their way out and head for Sibret, four miles southwest of Bastogne, where General Cota intended to reestablish the 28th Division headquarters. Strickler stayed at the command post with his staff until 11 p.m., destroying maps and equipment. Then they tried to find some tanks and armored cars to break through the German encirclement to the west, but every such vehicle had been either blown up by mines or destroyed by enemy tanks.

Strickler climbed into his jeep with a staff officer and his driver, and they roared down through a back alley to the outskirts of Wiltz, bullets flying all around them. On the edge of town they took a road to the west, but came under such heavy fire from mortars, machine guns and tanks that they had to abandon the jeep.

So Strickler and his two companions tried to make good their escape in the only way left them—on their feet and on their bellies, crawling into the woods outside town. Like thousands of GIs along the front, Strickler had become a straggler. His journey proved to be as desperate as Fuller's last-ditch stand in Clervaux, and as typical.

To evade the German units swarming all around them, the three men headed west on their 15-mile cross-country trek to Sibret. "It was cold and snowy," Strickler later recalled, "and we were all dead tired. Now and then we dropped to the ground and slept for ten minutes, usually to be awakened by the cold."

Nearing the village of Tarchamps at dawn on December

Makeshift defenders of Wiltz, members of the 28th Division's Band and Quartermaster Company regroup after having escaped the surrounded town. Joining with a pickup force of clerks, telephone linemen and stragglers, they held off German attacks on their division headquarters for two days, withdrawing only when they had run out of ammunition.

20, the stragglers heard the rumble of tanks and dropped to the ground just as a German panzer column dashed past them. By now they were ravenous, but they were afraid to go into the village to look for food. They hid in a wood all day and were joined there by more GIs and by about 50 Belgian civilians who were also fleeing from the Germans.

At dusk, the stragglers split up into small groups and veered southwestward across muddy fields crisscrossed by farmers' wire fences. Strickler had torn a piece of map off the wall at his command post in Wiltz, and with the aid of a luminous compass, he and his nine traveling companions made their way to the Bastogne-Arlon road, the main north-south artery, which they had to cross to reach Sibret. But this road, too, was jammed with German vehicles. Motorcycles were patrolling the highway, and guards were posted at intervals of about 300 yards.

Strickler and his group hid in a patch of woods until 3 a.m. Then, during a break in the German traffic, they rushed across the road and resumed their trek. They approached a village, but it was full of German tanks, and a pack of dogs chased them away. On reaching another village, Hollange, about five miles south of Bastogne, they were so desperately hungry that they risked prowling the streets in search of a friendly civilian who might give them food. But they found no one awake and hid in a barnyard haystack until dawn.

Then they knocked at a farmhouse door. A farmer appeared and indicated that German troops were sleeping inside. The Americans fled. Hardly had they reached a wooded hill overlooking the rural village when more than 100 German soldiers streamed out of a nearby sawmill and rode off on bicycles.

Strickler's hapless band hid again until nightfall and then struggled westward through the snow and a freezing drizzle. "We hit a stretch of Belgian wild land full of underbrush and dense pine forest," Strickler recalled later. "For hours we plowed our way through this stuff, having our eyes almost scratched out. It seemed almost hopeless. The boys were getting delirious, famished, fatigued and disgruntled. We had not seen a house all night. Suddenly we hit an open space, then a trail which led into a road to the village." Throwing caution to the wind, they proceeded right down the road into the settlement.

They knocked first at one house and then another, but no one answered. On their third attempt, a Belgian civilian opened his door. He fed the ravenous Americans steaming coffee, milk, bread, butter and jam. Their strength temporarily renewed, they started westward again.

Finally, about three and a half miles down the road, they were halted by American sentries, who took them into a building in the village of Vaux-les-Rosières. It turned out to be the headquarters of their own division, the 28th, whose staff had been driven out of Sibret the day before and had taken refuge here.

Strickler, who had been reported killed at Wiltz, received a warm welcome. "I was greeted like a ghost come to life," he said later. It was exactly three nights and three days since his odyssey had begun at Wiltz. Together with his companions, he lay down and enjoyed the first real sleep he had known in six nights.

While the remnants of the 28th Division were pulling back from Wiltz and Clervaux, disaster was befalling the 106th Division in the snowy forests high on the rugged Schnee Eifel. The 106th's plight, one of the worst defeats ever inflicted on a U.S. division, was to provoke controversy, recrimination and inconclusive investigations.

From its very formation, the 106th seemed to be haunted by bad luck. Activated in the U.S. in 1943, the division had undergone the standard infantry training and was ready for combat by early 1944. By then, however, American units already overseas were badly in need of individual replacements for the Normandy invasion and the subsequent fighting in Europe. As a result, the 106th—like other newly formed divisions—was cannibalized for replacements. Between April and August of 1944, some 7,247 men—60 per cent of the division's enlisted personnel—were transferred out and distributed among other units. Their places were taken by a motley collection of antiaircraft personnel, coast artillerymen, military policemen and transfers from the Army Specialized Training Program, bright young men who had been sent to college by the Army but had received little more than basic military training. These infusions brought the 106th back up to full strength, but the division never had a chance to develop the teamwork and *esprit* essential to effective performance in combat.

The 106th arrived in the Ardennes during the early part

Crosses mark the graves of American and German soldiers killed early in the Battle of the Bulge. This temporary cemetery in the Ardennes was set up by the Germans, who did not share the Americans' compunction about burying their own and the enemy dead in the same graveyard. After the War, the bodies were transferred to separate cemeteries.

of December. Its division headquarters was established at Saint-Vith, more than 10 miles behind the front, and two of its three regiments were sent to man the Schnee Eifel, the ridge protruding dangerously through Germany's West Wall defenses (map, page 92). To the north, the 422nd Regiment took up positions on a front that stretched more than four miles along the crest and eastern slope of the Schnee Eifel. And in the center, the 423rd Regiment held about five miles of the front, with one of its battalions curving around the extreme southern end of the Schnee Eifel in front of the village of Bleialf.

The valley of the Alf River separated the 423 from the division's other regiment, the 424th, which was deployed to the south of the division sector, covering a six-mile front.

The division commander, Major General Alan W. Jones, had disliked and distrusted his Schnee Eifel positions from the first. The 424th Regiment had the Our River at its back, leaving it little room for maneuver in case of attack. And the two regiments on the Schnee Eifel were in even more precarious positions. The roads running westward through the valleys at either end of the ridge converged at the village of Schönberg, eight miles due east of Saint-Vith. Attacking forces could therefore flow around both ends of

the Schnee Eifel and link up at Schönberg, trapping the forces on the ridge. The paved road from Schönberg to Saint-Vith would then be wide open.

Adding to the natural vulnerability of the 106th positions was the fact that both of the routes around the Schnee Eifel were only lightly held. The broad Losheim Gap was guarded only by one regiment of the 14th Cavalry Group, a small reconnaissance outfit that could be expected only to sound an alert in case of attack. At the southern end of the Schnee Eifel, the Alf River valley was held by a grab-bag assortment of units that included an antitank company, one platoon of a cannon company, a rifle platoon and a cavalry troop. If the Germans attacked, the 106th would get no meaningful help from either flank.

Still, General Jones understood that the Schnee Eifel had to be held. The Allied high command was planning a major offensive deep into Germany in the direction of Bonn. The Schnee Eifel represented an important breach in the West Wall, and it would make an excellent jumping-off point for the projected attack.

Jones's worst fears were realized on the first day of the German offensive. Making the most of Manteuffel's surprise tactics, two Volksgrenadier regiments surged through the

Losheim Gap, brushing past the 14th Cavalry Group. By midmorning the Germans were pushing down toward the village of Auw, three miles behind the northern flank of the 422nd Regiment. The garrison in Auw, a company of combat engineers, opened fire on the Germans. But the engineers were soon horrified by the sight of four huge Tigers lumbering toward them; the tanks belonged to the Führer Begleit Brigade—the sole exception to Manteuffel's decision to withhold his armor until after dark. Hopelessly outmatched, the engineers sniped away at the German infantrymen riding on the tops of the tanks. But the Tigers' 88mm guns swiveled around and started to pound the American positions.

Corporal Edward S. Withee saved one group of engineers from annihilation. "I'll stay," he shouted to his comrades, motioning to them to make a dash for safety. Opening fire on the tanks with a submachine gun, he managed to distract the tank gunners long enough for the rest to get away. Withee was quickly taken prisoner as the Germans completed the taking of Auw. The Germans now commanded the road to Schönberg.

Meanwhile, at the southern end of the Schnee Eifel, a regiment of Volksgrenadiers surged up the valley of the Alf River, overrunning the positions of the 423rd Regiment's antitank company and capturing most of the village of Bleialf. Later on, a force of miscellaneous GIs—engineers, quartermasters and headquarters troops—counterattacked and managed to recapture the village in house-to-house fighting. But they had staved off disaster only briefly: The 423rd had used up most of its reserves and ammunition. The pattern of the German advance now formed a fishhook around the southern end of the Schnee Eifel, threatening the exposed regiments from the south as well as the north.

Only a five-mile gap now separated the northern and southern arms of the rapidly closing German pincers.

Farther to the south, the 424th Regiment beat off attacks by an entire Volksgrenadier division during the morning hours of the 16th. But the German commander then ordered up his mobile reserve of bicycle troops supported by self-propelled guns. The Germans attacked toward the key road junction at Winterspelt and gained a strong foothold in the town. The capture of Winterspelt would pose a serious threat to Saint-Vith, only six miles to the northwest along a good macadam road.

All through the first day of the attack, General Jones kept in close touch with VIII Corps commander Middleton in Bastogne, and together they took what steps they could to stem the German tide. During the morning, Middleton had put Combat Command B of the 9th Armored Division at Jones's disposal, but the unit was stationed 12 miles north of Saint-Vith, and it would not arrive until the next morning. Jones himself tried to move up the reserve battalion of his 423rd Regiment from the Saint-Vith area. But in the confusion of battle, everything went wrong. The battalion pulled into Schönberg in the early afternoon and set up defenses around the village—only to be uprooted and moved farther forward to relieve the German pressure on the 422nd Regiment on the Auw-Schönberg road. Heading for its new position, the battalion piled back into trucks and took the wrong road in the darkness. It was after midnight when the GIs finally reached their assigned place, and by then they could do little but dig in.

By nightfall on the first day, the 106th was in grave peril. The 424th Regiment was being driven back to the Our River, and the two regiments on the Schnee Eifel were threatened with entrapment. Early that evening, General Middleton

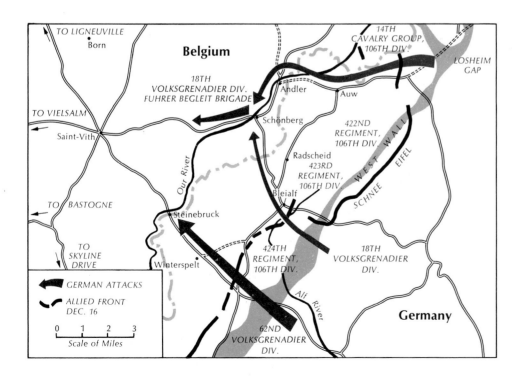

In the northern part of the Fifth Panzer Army's zone, a Volksgrenadier division and a panzer brigade circled the flanks of the Schnee Eifel, a ridge defended by two regiments of the 106th Infantry Division. These German drives converged at Schönberg, trapping the Americans on the ridge and opening the road to Saint-Vith. Meanwhile, a second Volksgrenadier division thrust northwest to Steinebrucke, pushing back the third regiment of the 106th.

called General Jones in Saint-Vith to express his concern about the two regiments on the ridge. Middleton reiterated the importance of the Schnee Eifel positions but said that unless the threatened flank in that area could be secured, the two regiments should be pulled out. Jones pondered the situation and then called Middleton back and tentatively suggested that the regiments be withdrawn. Middleton followed the accepted tradition of the U.S. Army and left the final decision on withdrawal up to the man on the spot.

Middleton also passed along some news that bore heavily on Jones's final decision. More help was en route to the 106th, Middleton said, in the form of a combat command of the 7th Armored Division. That unit, he said, should be arriving in Jones's area by 7 o'clock on the following morning, at roughly the same time as a platoon of tank destroyers from Combat Command B of the 9th Armored.

The fact is that the tanks of 7th Armored Division had to travel 70 miles from the border between Holland and Germany, and neither Jones nor Middleton realized that the unit could not possibly make it to the 106th Division's sector by 7 the next morning. It happened that a liaison officer from VIII Corps headquarters, Lieut. Colonel W. M. Slayden, was with Jones during the phone conversation with Middleton. Slayden doubted that the combat command would arrive by 7 a.m. but he did not speak up. "I should have said so," he explained later, "but that would have put me in the position of calling the corps commander a liar."

Fate had dealt General Jones a cruel hand. He had spent his whole professional life preparing in peacetime for combat, and now he was threatened with disaster on the first day of the enemy offensive. His reluctance to retreat during his division's first action was strengthened by a personal consideration. His son, Lieutenant Alan W. Jones Jr., was a staff officer with one of the trapped battalions of the 423rd Regiment. General Jones feared that if he ordered a retreat, it might look as though he had been influenced by a desire to save his son.

After long and anguished thought, Jones decided against withdrawal. He would put his faith in the reinforcements that were being rushed to his aid. He would send Combat Command B of the 9th Armored to aid the 424th Regiment in the Winterspelt area, and would commit the tanks of the 7th Armored in the Schnee Eifel area when they arrived.

During the night, the Germans worked feverishly to bring up reinforcements and to renew their two-pronged attack around the Schnee Eifel. At 6 a.m. on the 17th, the southern prong of Volksgrenadiers hit Bleialf again and broke through the American defenses. In the north, where the 14th Cavalry Group had withdrawn to a "final delaying position" and had then unaccountably withdrawn again, the Germans swept into the village of Andler and headed south for Schönberg. The gap between the pincer arms was rapidly closing, and the 7th Armored was still nowhere in sight. By half past eight, German forces converging from the north and south had linked up at Schönberg. The trap had snapped shut.

At 9:45 a.m., Jones sent the two surrounded regiments a message that promised help and raised the possibility of a retreat. "Expect to clear out area west of you this afternoon with reinforcements," Jones said. "Withdraw from present positions if they become untenable. Save all transportation possible."

Jones waited all morning, but the combat command of the 7th Armored did not appear; its advance elements were tied up in an immense traffic jam west of Saint-Vith. At 2:45

An American technician prepares to reinstall transmitter tubes at Radio Luxembourg, an Allied propaganda station. On December 19, when German troops advanced to within a few miles of the station, the transmitters were dismantled and removed to prevent the enemy from using the station—which went back on the air after the German threat had faded.

p.m., the general sent both of his trapped regiments orders to fall back to the west bank of the Our River, behind Schönberg and Andler. But radio traffic was so heavy that this message was not received by the regiments until after midnight. It was then superseded by another message—transmitted from 106th Division headquarters at 2:15 a.m. and received by the regiments at 4 a.m.—instructing the 422nd and the 423rd to attack enemy panzer concentrations along the road between Schönberg and Saint-Vith and then move into positions protecting Saint-Vith from the east. The message promised airdrops of food, ammunition and water to the beleaguered regiments.

When Colonel George L. Descheneaux Jr., the commander of the 422nd, read this message, he bowed his head and said in despair, "My poor men, they'll be cut to pieces." An attack by his trapped outfit was all but suicidal. The men were running out of ammunition and medical supplies. They were being called upon to make their way over rugged, unfamiliar terrain and attack panzers. But orders were orders; Descheneaux's outfit and Colonel Charles C. Cavender's 423rd got ready to attack early on December 18.

The regiments moved out at about 9 a.m., after destroying their field kitchens (the food supply was nearly exhausted in any case) and other excess equipment and leaving their wounded behind in the care of aid men. Rain and fog enveloped the area, and many units were soon lost or stranded in the woods. Cavender's regiment ran into enemy troops along the Bleialf-Schönberg road and pushed the Germans back; the GIs then advanced to within 1,000 yards of Schönberg and dug in for the night.

Descheneaux's regiment picked its way toward a designated hill in a wooded area only a mile and a half from Schönberg. The weary, dispirited men stumbled over the gullies and ravines, slipping and sliding through the mud and slush, and wound up in a patch of woods three miles from their objective. The men did not realize they were in the wrong place.

Meanwhile, the promised airdrops were strangled in red tape. The initial request had been forwarded directly to the IX Tactical Air Command by an officer at VIII Corps. The air command loaded cargo planes with available ammunition and medical supplies and prepared to carry out the mission. But no provision had been made for a fighter escort or for proper base facilities. By the time the Air Force and Army got around to taking corrective action, the battle was over.

On the morning of December 19, the two regiments tried to pull themselves together for an attack toward Schönberg. Descheneaux's men moved out of their patch of woods at about 10 a.m., believing the objective to be only about a mile away. As they neared the Bleialf-Auw road, they came under heavy fire from German machine guns and tanks. In the ensuing confusion, one battalion ended up in a fire fight with nearby elements of Cavender's regiment. Other elements of the 422nd were overrun by German tanks.

To Descheneaux, the situation was hopeless. His men were hemmed in on all sides and were being raked by German machine-gun fire. Casualties were pouring into an aid station next to his command post, and he could hear the screams and moans of the wounded men.

Descheneaux came to a painful conclusion: he would have to surrender the regiment. He sent his executive officer, Lieut. Colonel Frederick W. Nagle, under a white flag to a German antiaircraft unit nearby. Said Nagle later: "That was the hardest thing I ever had to do. The worst part was coming back and telling the men how and where they should surrender. Many of them didn't understand it; they wanted to fight on."

With Descheneaux's approval, about 400 men of one battalion tried to make their way out to the southwest. But after two days, they too were surrounded and forced to surrender. Another group was stopped by a minefield near Bleialf. All together, fewer than 150 men out of 800 straggled through to the American lines.

Colonel Cavender's regiment suffered a similar fate. Early on December 19, while the regiment was assembling for the attack toward Schönberg, it came under heavy fire from German artillery along the Bleialf-Schönberg road. German infantry overran the 423rd's supporting field-artillery battalion. Even so, one infantry battalion moved out toward Schönberg and reached the outskirts of the town. But the Germans turned their antiaircraft guns on the GIs of the attacking battalion, poured a hail of fire into them and drove them back. Another battalion made a weak and fruitless attack. The remaining battalion had meanwhile strayed off and been lost in the fog; this was the unit that engaged in the fire fight with the 422nd Regiment.

Ringed around by Germans, Colonel Cavender reached the same decision as Colonel Descheneaux: he would save his men from almost certain slaughter by surrendering. The Germans rounded up scattered men of both regiments. In the flush of victory, they did not stop to count the prisoners. But at least 7,000 GIs were marched off into Germany.

The remaining regiment of the 106th Division, the 424th, very nearly met with disaster too. At dawn on December 17, German infantrymen renewed their attack on the southern flank of the 106th, driving the last elements of the 424th out of Winterspelt. The bridge over the Our at Steinebruck—the main crossing point on the road between Winterspelt and Saint-Vith—now lay only two miles from the enemy advance guards. If the Germans got there first, the 424th would be stranded hopelessly on the east bank.

The Volksgrenadiers pushed their way forward as far as a saddle overlooking Steinebruck, sending one battalion reeling back in disorder and threatening to overrun the regiment's left flank. But a hastily assembled task force managed to hold the flank and prevent the Germans from taking the Steinebruck bridge.

The Germans also came close to breaking through on the regiment's right flank. One small-unit attack was repelled when Private First Class Henry S. Litchfield mowed down 10 Germans with a Browning automatic rifle he took from a wounded comrade. Another attack was staved off by Private First Class Harry V. Arvannis, a mortarman who propped a damaged weapon between his knees and sent a shell crashing among a dozen charging Germans. Arvannis then killed two more Germans with his pistol and put a third one out of action by hitting him in the face with the weapon.

While the men of the 424th held an outpost in front of the Our River, Combat Command B of the 9th Armored Division arrived as scheduled and went into action in the early morning of the 17th. The unit's commander, Brigadier General William M. Hoge, rushed his armored infantry battalion across the river, overcame heavy German resistance and seized the high ground around Winterspelt.

Hoge then ordered his infantry to dig in while he brought up his tanks for an attack on Winterspelt. At that point, however, he received word from General Jones to pull back across the Our during the night. With American resistance crumbling on the Schnee Eifel, a counterattack against Winterspelt no longer made sense. Hoge ordered his tanks to halt their advance and instructed his infantrymen to wait for darkness before withdrawing across the river.

That night, the two battalions of the 424th Regiment withdrew safely across the Our, where they joined Hoge's waiting tanks. On the river's west bank, the two outfits hastily established a new front line nearly four miles long, together with advance guards of the 7th Armored Division, just then arriving to the north. These units were all that stood between the advancing Germans and their next objective: Saint-Vith.

Manteuffel's Fifth Panzer Army had won tremendous victories in the opening phase of his offensive, destroying the 106th Division and shattering the 28th Division. Yet, as Manteuffel realized, the victories had been won at a high cost in time. He had planned to capture both Saint-Vith and Bastogne by the end of the second day, December 17. But on that night, Colonel Fuller's regiment of the 28th was still holding out in the Clervaux area, and Colonel Strickler did not abandon Wiltz until the night of December 19. Even the ill-fated 106th Division managed to hold out until December 19, tying up German units that had urgent assignments farther to the west.

Fierce fighting by outnumbered and outmanuevered GIs had granted the American command time to defend two key road junctions in the path of Manteuffel's army: Saint-Vith and Bastogne.

THE ALL-PURPOSE ENGINEERS

Preparing to blow up a Belgian railway bridge in the path of onrushing Germans, three U.S. Army engineers emplace TNT charges while a fourth stands guard.

FROM SUPPORT TROOPS TO FRONTLINE FIGHTERS

Watching helplessly on December 18 as a bridge spanning Belgium's Lienne Creek was blown up in his face, SS panzer leader Joachim Peiper pounded his knee in fury and muttered, "The damned engineers! The damned engineers!" Peiper's curse was a well-earned compliment for the U.S. Army engineers, who turned up again and again to thwart German forces during the Battle of the Bulge.

Like the men of other services, the engineers were engaged in routine work on the eve of battle—reconnoitering and mapping the terrain, quarrying rock for road building, operating sawmills to provide lumber for winter shelters, purifying drinking water. The instant the German offensive struck, they threw all their energies into efforts to block the panzer columns. Besides blowing bridges, they barricaded and mined roads vital to the German tanks. They also fought as infantry, defending critical positions until reinforcements arrived. In the Stavelot area, three units of engineers held their ground so stubbornly that Major General James M. Gavin of the 82nd Airborne Division rated them "as effective as a good combat division."

When the Americans mustered the strength to counterattack, engineers were in the forefront, moving up with the infantry and armor. They toiled night and day to replace destroyed bridges, and to make roads passable and keep them that way in spite of snow, ice and the German shelling. They risked their lives to clear paths through minefields. And again, as on the defense, the engineers did their job under enemy fire; their urgent work rarely allowed them the luxury of taking cover.

Yet for all their labors, their hard-won successes and the heavy casualties they sustained, the engineers still had to put up with the gibes of the infantrymen—whether ignorant newcomers or wisecracking veterans who refused to forget the old rivalry between the services. An engineer outfit would trail in from the front line filthy and exhausted after fighting for days—only to hear some infantryman say, "Why the hell don't you rear-echelon bastards ever come up front and fight?"

An engineer equips a jeep's front wheel with a "mud shoe," improvised by his company to give vehicles better traction in deep snow and mud.

A dead engineer is still seated upright at the wheel of his truck, machine-gunned by a strafing German plane near the front line in the Luxembourg Ardennes.

Expecting to be attacked, an engineer mans a .30-caliber machine gun near a concealed tank.

Weary engineers emerge from a wood near Wiltz after an all-night fight to beat off an infantry assault.

HOLDING THE LINE WITH GRENADES AND CHICANERY

The engineers often worked, as one of them noted, "under the very noses" of the SS. They were not equipped for heavy fighting, but when a German unit attacked them, the engineers had no choice but to return fire with their rifles and light ma-

Sent sprawling by German snipers, members of the 202nd Combat Engineers return fire from openings in a wall. A discarded mine detector lies at their right.

chine guns. Because their last-minute efforts to seal off roads and bridges tended to leave them isolated from the retreating American units, they frequently lacked artillery support.

Out of necessity, they also fought with brazen trickery. To fool the enemy into believing that weak units were too strong to be attacked, engineers scurried from point to point at top speed, firing rifles and

tossing grenades. One officer ordered his five trucks to drive up to the front lines with lights on, then to the rear with lights off; by repeating the round trip all through the night, the drivers gave the Germans the misleading impression that reinforcements were arriving in droves.

The spunk and stamina of some American engineers was awesome. A lone engineer maintained a frigid lookout on a

mountaintop near Malmédy for 28 hours before being relieved. Another, using a bazooka for the first time, held his fire until an approaching German tank was only 10 yards away. He was blinded by the explosion that knocked out the tank, which left him nearly helpless as a German machine gun let loose nearby. But the engineer judged the gun's position by sound and silenced it with a grenade.

CLEARING MINES AND LAYING MINEFIELDS

"Delousing" was the graphic term the engineers gave to the dangerous task of finding and neutralizing any concealed mines. The snows in the Ardennes added to the hazards of the job, covering visual clues to buried mines and frequently weakening the signals from magnetic mine detectors.

Worse, the metal detectors were utterly useless for locating the numerous German mines encased in wood or plastic. When the engineers suspected that an area was seeded with such nonmetal devices, they could make sure only by crawling forward carefully and probing by hand for mines hidden beneath the snow.

The engineers were also responsible for laying minefields of their own and otherwise delaying the enemy with felled trees and barbed wire. The task of burying the mines in frozen ground was brutal as well as time-consuming, especially when only pickaxes were available. But with the aid of jackhammers, the engineers of one corps managed to lay 80,000 mines in a month, and in the same span of time a single battalion of engineers studded 12 square miles with mines.

Mining a road, an engineer lowers a 10-pound antitank charge into a hole and prepares to scoop dirt over it. Sometimes two mines were buried together to increase chances of disabling a heavily armored Tiger tank.

Engineers carrying mine detectors cautiously probe a snowy road five miles southeast of Vielsalm. In a dense minefield, engineers often exploded "snakes"—tubes filled with TNT that set off mines for seven feet around.

Struggling through a blizzard, engineers string up barbed wire to obstruct German infantrymen. To make it dangerous for the Germans to cut through such barriers, engineers linked explosive charges to the wires.

THE STRUGGLE FOR CONTROL OF THE ROADS

In the rugged, heavily wooded Ardennes, control of the highways was essential—both to keep American armor and infantry moving, and to stem the German advance. Creating roadblocks was relatively easy; a single engineer could quickly interdict a road by felling trees with explosive charges or by laying a "daisy chain"—a string of antitank mines stretched across a road. But it was hard work to make rutted or swampy roads passable for the American tanks and truck convoys.

Engineer road crews struggled to level the roadbeds with tons of crushed rock or rows of logs. They bulldozed disabled vehicles off the road or dragged the wrecks aside with truck winches. Where the Germans had built log roadblocks, engineers usually cleared the way with TNT. Even so, the task could be time-consuming. One engineer unit needed a full day to clear away an enemy barricade that contained 35 thick tree trunks.

Opening a blocked road, an engineer employs a bulldozer to topple a German armored vehicle into the woods. Lacking bulldozers, engineers often called on tanks to clear debris.

A First Army engineer employs wire and cord to bind dozens of half-pound charges of TNT to the side of a tree destined to be knocked down for building a roadblock.

As an ambulance waits, a bulldozer operator from the 202nd Combat Engineers repairs a bomb-damaged road by plowing earth from an embankment into the crater.

Members of the 202nd Combat Engineers employ a two-and-a-half-ton truck to plow a snow-covered road.

The 249th Combat Engineers spread branches

To lend traction on a curve, men of the 166th Combat Engineers shovel sand into a spreading machine.

Lacking plows, the 178th Combat Engineers

of evergreens to prevent snow from drifting.

A snowed-in airstrip near Bastogne is plowed out by a bulldozer operator of the 159th Combat Engineers.

use shovels to clear a road near Bastogne.

A cloud of snow and ice erupts as the 276th Combat Engineers resort to dynamite to clear packed snow.

INGENIOUS WAYS OF COMBATING ICE AND SNOW

Once in firm control of a road, engineers had to work round the clock to maintain it. A number of engineer units, lacking proper snowplows for their standard two-and-a-half-ton trucks, fashioned blades out of whatever scrap metal came to hand. Some ingenious tinkerers even worked out elaborate systems for angling their make-shift plows to suit road conditions and the depth of the snow.

Engineers also improvised crude but ef-fective machines for spreading sand and gravel after each snowfall. One company, lacking a sand-spreading vehicle, attached a radiator fan horizontally to the rear axle of a captured German truck, then weld-ed a cone on top. As the vehicle moved slowly along, engineers shoveled sand into the cone, and the rotating fan dispersed it across the road.

One engineer stands guard while another readies a bridge in Malmédy for destruction with some 850 pounds of TNT. The white tape attached to the stone walls on either side of the bridge was a standard warning sign.

Building a span over a stream, members of the 49th Engineer Combat Battalion lay a wooden support structure for a trestle bridge. The treadway bridge in the background served as a temporary solution.

DYNAMITING BRIDGES— AND REBUILDING THEM

In keeping with their adage, "Dynamite is the enemy of movement," engineers never skimped on TNT when destroying bridges in the panzers' path. To ensure the razing of long spans, they would use up to 1,000 tons of TNT. They worked fast: One company readied eight bridges for demolition in a single day. But engineers did not blow bridges until the last minute, knowing they would have to be rebuilt for counterattack.

Destroying bridges was easy. Building bridges in winter was a terrible ordeal. To lay foundations, engineers waded in deep, icy waters. Wood froze so hard that nails could barely be driven into it. The heavy metal panels of Bailey bridges sometimes slipped and crushed hands and feet.

Yet the construction went on—and it proceeded almost as speedily as did the bridge-blowing operations. On the Ourthe River, the 294th Combat Engineers started work on a 180-foot steel bridge around midnight on December 31 and in spite of all hazards were finished and ready for a New Year's celebration at 6 a.m.

On December 19, Eisenhower met with his top field commanders at Verdun to formulate a strategy to halt the Germans. The Allied situation, bleak from the start, appeared to be getting worse by the hour: Peiper's panzers were racing unchecked to the west; Manteuffel's legions were pouring through a 30-mile gap between Saint-Vith and Bastogne. Rumors were rife of German paratroopers landing at every crossroad and of enemy commandos disguised in American uniforms popping up behind every bush. Back home, apprehensive Americans were wondering how the tide of battle in Europe could have been reversed so suddenly when victory seemed so near.

But Eisenhower injected a note of optimism when he sat down with his commanders around a table in a dank old French military barracks. "The present situation," Eisenhower told his solemn generals, "is to be regarded as one of opportunity for us and not of disaster. There will be only cheerful faces at this conference table."

General Patton grinned and said, "Hell, let's have the guts to let the sons of bitches go all the way to Paris. Then we'll really cut 'em off and chew 'em up!"

"No," Eisenhower responded quietly. "The enemy will never be allowed to cross the Meuse."

The generals adopted a simple strategy of containment and counterattack, learned during World War I and taught thereafter in American service schools. Advantageous conditions were already developing; the 2nd and 99th Infantry Divisions at Elsenborn Ridge and the 4th Infantry Division and a portion of the 10th Armored Division near Echternach were anchoring the broken ends of the American front in the north and the south respectively. From these anchors, U.S. forces would build strong positions outward along both flanks of the enemy salient, restricting the breakthrough to a narrow corridor; then they would sever the corridor and cut off the enemy troops heading for the Meuse. The counterattack, Eisenhower decided, would be launched initially against the Germans' southern flank by Patton's Third Army, whose headquarters lay 50 miles to the southeast in the city of Nancy. As Patton's troops sliced northward through the German flank, they were to relieve the Belgian town of Bastogne, a vital and gravely threatened road center.

Eisenhower turned to Patton and asked him when he

4

The Americans map a counterattack
Patton's startling boast
The jolt of "seeing American soldiers running away"
A traffic jam 12 miles long
The Germans' "bouncing ball" assaults
From a horseshoe defense line to a fortified goose egg
A lifesaving change in the weather
An execution stayed by a friendly innkeeper
Private Goldstein's challenge to a panzer brigade
The mystery of the Stavelot bridge
A grim legacy of murder

BATTLE FOR SAINT-VITH

would be able to attack. "On December 22, with three divisions," Patton replied.

The other generals stirred in disbelief. Patton, always attack-minded, had surely gone too far this time. He was proposing a movement of enormous size and complexity, requiring him to pull three divisions out of line, wheel them northward and launch an assault—all in three days.

Patton, enjoying the attention, lighted up a cigar and pointed to the German penetrations on a map. "This time the Kraut has stuck his head in a meat grinder," he said in his high voice. "And this time I've got hold of the handle." In fact, Patton said, he had already drawn up three plans the Third Army might use in the current crisis; he had only to telephone his chief of staff, Brigadier General Hobart R. Gay, to set in motion the plan that called for a thrust toward Bastogne.

As Patton left the meeting to make his call, Eisenhower accompanied him to the door. "Funny thing, George," the Supreme Commander said, "every time I get another star, I get attacked." The new five-star general had received his fourth star in early 1943, just before American forces were hit hard by Field Marshal Erwin Rommel's Afrika Korps at the Kasserine Pass in Tunisia. Patton, who had been called in to revitalize the troops on that occasion, slyly reminded his superior, "And every time you get attacked, Ike, I have to bail you out."

Later that evening, Eisenhower pondered the need for another change in the command structure in the Ardennes. The German attack had driven a wedge through the American forces and was playing havoc with communications between the First and Ninth Armies in the north and the Third Army in the south. The headquarters of General Bradley, the man in charge of these armies, was in the city of Luxembourg, far to the southeast of his First Army. This meant that Bradley would have to make a day-long trip around the burgeoning German salient in order to supervise the defense in the north. The journey would be perilous for Bradley and perhaps also for his armies, which might need a snap decision from him while he was in transit.

Eisenhower's intelligence officer, Major General Kenneth W. D. Strong, suggested sensibly that Bradley's command be split, with Field Marshal Montgomery, the senior field commander closest to the threat on the north, taking tem-porary control of the First and Ninth Armies and Bradley remaining in charge of Patton's Third Army in the south. Eisenhower realized that such a move might seem to discredit Bradley; he also knew that it would distress the many American officers who considered Monty arrogant, condescending and too cautious in waging war. But the proposal made good sense—and not just as a way to guarantee tighter control of the action. It might also encourage Montgomery to commit British reserves to the battle.

After weighing the pros and cons, Eisenhower decided the following morning in favor of the split. As expected, Bradley protested the loss of half his command. The decision was a bitter one for him, but when he saw that Ike was adamant, he accepted it with better grace than a number of his fellow officers did.

For his part, Montgomery did little to help matters when he paid his first visit to First Army headquarters near Liège later that same day. Jauntily attired in a beret and brimming with self-confidence, he stepped briskly into the headquarters—"like Christ come to cleanse the temple," one of his own aides observed.

"Well, gentlemen," Montgomery said to the glum First Army staff, "I gather that a difficult situation has arisen. Now do tell me the form."

On being shown a detailed map used by the First Army operations staff, Monty ignored it and instead consulted a small map prepared by his own staff officers, who had been visiting the front for the past few days. Later, when asked to lunch with the First Army commander, General Hodges, he declined the invitation, produced a wicker picnic basket and sat munching a sandwich by himself. It happened that Montgomery was in the habit of eating alone. But the First Army officers, who were unaware of that fact, construed his behavior as a deliberate affront. Their bitterness increased.

In spite of the friction between Montgomery and the Americans, the command change had an immediate payoff. As Eisenhower had hoped, Monty now dispatched the British XXX Corps to back up the tank units that he had already deployed to protect key bridges across the Meuse. He was still too cautious for American tastes, urging the withdrawal of U.S. troops from exposed positions, including the town of Saint-Vith—to "tidy up the battlefield," as he put it. But he proved willing to listen to the Americans. When they strenuously objected to any withdrawal from Saint-Vith, Montgomery chose not to press the point.

Sound reasons supported the Americans' argument for making a stand at Saint-Vith. Field commanders on both sides considered it a key to the struggle for the northern sector of the Ardennes. Whoever possessed the town controlled the meeting point of no fewer than six paved highways. Initially the panzers—using the blitzkrieg tactic of bypassing centers of resistance—had swept past Saint-Vith to the north and south. But the farther their spearheads traveled, the more the Germans needed to oust the enemy from Saint-Vith: with the road hub in American hands, they would never be able to ferry enough supplies forward to their front-running elements.

The chief responsibility for defending Saint-Vith lay with the 7th Armored Division—an outfit that found itself in the town more by frustrating happenstance than by design. Ordered to the Ardennes on the first day of the German offensive, the 7th Armored had hurriedly pulled out of position in the Aachen area and rumbled away to the south.

At 11 a.m. on December 17, the vanguard of the division, Combat Command B, reached the Belgian town of Vielsalm, stopped to refuel, and then wheeled eastward toward Saint-Vith and the maelstrom of combat beyond. By then, the 7th Armored had been assigned a rescue mission: to push through Saint-Vith to Schönberg, opening an escape corridor for the two regiments of the 106th Division trapped on the Schnee Eifel. The beleaguered regiments were then in desperate shape—cut off, surrounded and running out of ammunition. The commander of the 106th, General Jones, was pinning all his hopes for their survival on the timely intervention of the 7th Armored.

But when the lead units of the 7th Armored left Vielsalm on the road to Saint-Vith, they ran into a choking mass of traffic headed the other way. Supply trucks, rear-echelon units of the 106th Division, VIII Corps artillery and units of the routed 14th Cavalry Group were all struggling frantically to get out of the combat zone. Near the village of Poteau, a tidal wave of westbound traffic swamped the GIs.

Slowly, yard by yard, the 7th Armored units pushed forward against the tide. Clearing the way was Major Donald P. Boyer Jr., operations officer of the 38th Armored Infantry

Battalion. "It was a case of every dog for himself," he later said in disgust. "It wasn't orderly; it wasn't military; it wasn't a pretty sight. We were seeing American soldiers running away." And it got worse. "About a mile up the road at the little town of Petit Thier, all traffic had stopped. In fact it was the most perfect traffic jam I have ever seen. . . . Several times senior officers in command cars attempted to pull into a space which I was opening up, and each time I told them to get back, that I didn't care who they were. Nothing was coming through except our tanks."

In a cold rage, Boyer ordered his Sherman tank to the head of the column. When a weapons carrier refused to move aside, Boyer told his driver to charge; the weapons carrier swerved into a ditch just in time to avoid being crushed. "If anyone gets in the way," Boyer yelled, "run over the son of a bitch."

"Go get 'em, Major!" shouted a GI. "Give 'em hell!" A sergeant leaped out of an artillery jeep that was headed for the rear. "I'm going with those damned tanks," he called to his companions. "I joined this Army to fight, not to run!" He clambered up behind the turret of an eastbound tank.

The Germans missed a golden opportunity by failing to attack Saint-Vith on December 17, while the vanguard of the 7th Armored was still struggling to get there; all day the only defenders were a few engineer units and miscellaneous outfits. The lead tanks of the 7th Armored did not reach the town until well after nightfall. The division commander, Brigadier General Robert W. Hasbrouck, thereupon reluctantly called a halt. He then had less than a third of his division on hand, and the continuing snarl of traffic, complicated by darkness, made it senseless to try and push

any farther. His unavoidable decision sealed the fate of the two trapped 106th Division regiments. They held out until their ammunition, food and drink were exhausted. Then on December 19 they surrendered to the Germans.

During the night, the defenses of Saint-Vith continued to strengthen. More and more units from the front, including the remaining regiment of the 106th Division and a combat command of the 9th Armored Division, fell back on the town, and the rest of the 7th Armored rolled in from the west. In the hours of darkness, a horseshoe-shaped defense line gradually took form around Saint-Vith, stretching for 15 miles.

On the morning of December 18, the Germans tested the hastily formed perimeter, employing what Hasbrouck called the bouncing-ball method—striking first in one place and then another. In all, they hit four widely spaced positions on the rim of the American horseshoe—at one point threatening to outflank the defenders, at another penetrating the center of the line. Though Hasbrouck was short of manpower, he juggled his troops masterfully, dispatching them here and there to meet each new German threat as it arose. The Germans were repeatedly forced to fall back, leaving behind them the smoking hulks of tanks and the scattered hummocks of dead infantrymen, dark against the white, frozen fields. On December 19, the defenders were further buttressed by the arrival from the southeast of the retreating 112th Infantry Regiment, which had been separated from the rest of the 28th Division. The German jabs continued on that day and the next, but they seemed strangely feeble.

The Germans, in fact, were having serious traffic problems of their own. The stubborn American resistance at

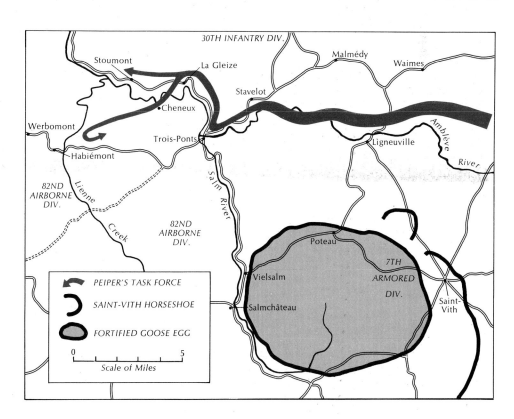

At the Belgian town of Namur during the Battle of the Bulge, a British tank guards the Meuse River against an expected attack by the Germans. Field Marshal Montgomery on December 19 had deployed tanks and armored cars to hold the bridges along a 60-mile stretch of the Meuse. But he confessed that his notion of the attack route the Germans would use was "unpleasantly vague."

Deployed in a horseshoe-shaped perimeter, the U.S. 7th Armored Division and supporting units defended Saint-Vith for three days, then pulled back into the shaded oval between Saint-Vith and Vielsalm. Threatened with entrapment, they then withdrew through the lines of the 82nd Airborne Division. To the north, Joachim Peiper's task force rolled west (red arrow) to Trois-Ponts, and then—after detouring around two blown bridges—to the La Gleize area. There his troops were cut off by the U.S. 30th Infantry and 82nd Airborne Divisions.

Elsenborn Ridge had forced the attackers there to sideslip to the south. As a result, General Dietrich's troops and tanks were tangled up with units of Manteuffel's army, and huge traffic jams were delaying the big blow at Saint-Vith.

By the evening of December 20, the German High Command had lost patience with the fitful sallies against the Saint-Vith horseshoe; American control of the road hub was stalling the entire Fifth Army offensive toward the Meuse. An all-out attack by the available elements of two infantry divisions and a tank brigade was ordered for the next day.

At 11 a.m. on December 21, the Germans laid down a massive artillery bombardment on the Saint-Vith perimeter and then hurled wave upon wave of tanks and infantry at the Americans. Time and again the defenders managed to hold their ground against overwhelming odds. The Germans, thoroughly frustrated by nightfall, mounted three more major attacks—from the south, east and north, each along a main road into town.

Major Boyer, who a few days earlier had bucked retreating Americans to get 7th Armored tanks forward to Saint-Vith, found himself caught up in the action at the apex of the horseshoe. "The Krauts kept boring in, no matter how fast we decimated their assault squads," he later wrote. "Again and again there was a flare of flame and smoke as some Kraut got in close enough to heave a grenade into a machine-gun crew or launch a dread *Panzerfaust*. One caliber .50 squad which had been dishing out a deadly hail of fire was hit by a *Panzerfaust*, which struck the barrel halfway between the breech and muzzle. The gunner fell forward on the gun with half his face torn off; the loader had his left arm torn off at the shoulder and was practically decapitated; while the gun commander was tossed about 15 feet away from the gun to lie there quite still.

"Whenever a machine-gun crew was killed off, other men leaped from their holes to take over the gun. . . . Always there were more Germans, and more Germans, and then more Germans—attacking, attacking and reattacking for better than one and a half hours."

As Boyer watched, German tanks loomed up in the darkness on the crest of a hill, and five American Shermans came out of nowhere to challenge them. The Germans fired a point-blank salvo of white flares. Blinded by the intense light, the American tankers groped about helplessly and were knocked off one by one. From the way the German tanks later roared past him in the dark, Boyer guessed—correctly—that they were equipped with some new kind of infrared viewer that allowed their drivers to see at night.

By 8 p.m. the American lines had been pierced in at least three places; the command post of Boyer's superior, Lieut. Colonel William H. G. Fuller, had been overwhelmed, and Fuller had had to make his own exit to the rear. Of the original 1,142 men in his 38th Armored Infantry Battalion, only 100 were still in condition to fight. At least eight Panther and Tiger tanks were rolling through the streets of Saint-Vith, and German infantrymen were pouring in behind. The Americans could no longer contain the attack. Word came down from Brigadier General Bruce C. Clarke, commander of the 7th Armored's Combat Command B: "Save what vehicles you can; attack to the west; we are forming a new line west of town." Similar messages went out to the other beleaguered units in the horseshoe.

Boyer worked his way down the lines, relaying the order. Then he led his 100 survivors west through the forest in a raging snowstorm. Discovering that his unit was nearly surrounded, he told the men to split up into groups of five and try to slip through the Germans in the dark.

The following morning, Boyer and the four men in his own little group, stumbling through snow that came up almost to their knees, approached a busy main road out of Saint-Vith. Boyer decided to wait until it was dark before trying to sneak across the open highway. He motioned his men toward a hiding place—a stone wall on a hill overlooking the road. But as one soldier crawled forward, he loosened a rock that tumbled onto the road below. In an instant they heard Germans shouting, and one voice called out in English, telling the Americans that they were surrounded and that they had better come out or they would be blasted by mortar fire. Boyer realized that it would be suicidal to fight. He stood up slowly and climbed down the hill. A German officer was waiting for him with a smile. "Just the fortunes of war," the German said sympathetically. "Maybe I'll be a prisoner tomorrow."

As the American forces in the shattered horseshoe pulled back to regroup west of Saint-Vith, a message arrived for General Hasbrouck from Major General Matthew B. Ridg-

THE HIGH COST OF COLD FEET

During the Battle of the Bulge, more than 15,000 American soldiers were disabled by frostbitten feet or trench foot. The afflictions were quite similar: cold—accompanied by moisture in the case of trench foot—slowed circulation in the foot and killed tissue. Sometimes gangrene set in and the foot had to be amputated.

The U.S. Army had developed preventive footgear—insulated shoepacs *(below)* that would have helped had they been available in time. And the GIs had been taught to change to dry socks often and to massage their feet whenever possible to keep up circulation. But such measures were often impossible in combat.

Under treatment for trench foot, a victim raises and exposes his feet.

A GI dons his shoepacs—rubber-bound boots with leather tops and felt insoles. Shoepac shipments did not begin arriving until late January.

way, commander of the newly arrived XVIII Airborne Corps, which had established a line still farther west with the 82nd Airborne Division. Ridgway outlined his scheme for a defense perimeter between Saint-Vith and Vielsalm—a rough oval nearly 10 miles across *(map, page 113)*. This area, soon dubbed the "fortified goose egg," was to be held by Hasbrouck's troops and supplied by airdrops until reinforcements could be sent.

Neither Hasbrouck nor Clarke liked the idea. Their troops were spread out and exhausted. Moreover, the goose egg contained a dense forest and only one decent road—hardly ideal terrain for a mobile armored defense. Sarcastically, Clarke called the operation "Custer's Last Stand." That label almost proved prophetic.

Even as the oval perimeter took form, the Germans began piercing it at will, penetrating deep on the north flank. By midmorning on December 22, Hasbrouck realized that his men would not be able to hold out much longer and sent an urgent message to Ridgway: "In my opinion if we don't get out of here before night, we will not have a 7th Armored Division left."

Ridgway considered Hasbrouck unduly pessimistic and wanted him to stick it out in the goose egg. But now, Montgomery felt compelled to intervene as the commander in the north. Of the 22,000 troops at Saint-Vith, 6,000 had already been killed or wounded, and Monty saw no point in subjecting the Americans to further loss. He ordered a withdrawal, adding a tribute to the defenders of Saint-Vith: "They can come back with all honor. They come back to the more secure positions. They put up a wonderful show."

In his command post at a schoolhouse in Vielsalm, Hasbrouck worked out the details of the retreat. The troops, loaded aboard hundreds of trucks, half-tracks and tanks, would pull out in the early morning hours of December 23 through a narrow escape corridor held open by the 82nd Airborne Division in the west. The plan looked good on paper, but was made questionable by a sudden thaw that turned the dirt roads into quagmires. General Clarke reported that, on a tour of the perimeter, his jeep had sunk over the hubcaps in the mud.

At 5 o'clock on the morning of December 23, Clarke's command post received a call from Lieut. Colonel Robert Erlenbusch, who was trying desperately to shore up the American defenses against attacks from the northeast. "There's a fire fight just to the south of me," Erlenbusch reported. "We've got to get out now!" Clarke told him to hold on for another 10 minutes while he made up his mind. He dreaded starting the mass retreat on the muddy roads, where slowed or stranded vehicles would be sitting ducks for German artillery.

Clarke hung up and went outdoors. He was surprised to discover that a stinging-cold wind had begun blowing in from the east, and his spirits surged when he stepped onto the rutted road outside the command post. A few hours earlier, the road had been an impassable ooze; now its surface was hard as a rock.

Clarke rushed back inside and called Hasbrouck. "A miracle has happened, General!" he exclaimed. "That cold snap that's hit us has frozen the roads. I think we can make it now. At 0600 I'm going to start to move." Then Erlen-

busch called in again. "Sir . . ." he pleaded. Clarke interrupted him: "All right, Bob, crank up!"

Throughout the goose egg, motors roared to life and vehicles started moving over the quick-frozen roads and fields. With a 7th Armored task force covering their retreat, the defenders of Saint-Vith slowly streamed over the Salm River to safety behind the 82nd Airborne's lines. Bruce Clarke stood in a field directing traffic. He looked at his men as they went by: they were dirty, unshaven, red-eyed and gaunt, and he was proud of every one. When the last truck had passed, Clarke climbed heavily into his own jeep and told his driver to bring up the rear of the column. He had not slept lying down for seven days; now, as his jeep bounced down the rutted road, he fell fast asleep.

Although Saint-Vith was lost, the 7th Armored Division and its supporting units had succeeded in tying up an entire enemy corps for nearly a week, disrupting the Germans' timetable and blocking supply routes crucial to their race for the Meuse. And the Allies were now flooding the Ardennes with reinforcements.

By the time the fortified goose egg collapsed, British tank units were guarding the Meuse bridges, while just to the east of the river the U.S. VII Corps was assembling for an eventual counterattack. On the northern flank to the east of the 82nd Airborne, the U.S. 30th Infantry Division had moved into blocking positions along the Amblève River in the vicinity of Malmédy.

The deployment of the 30th Division along the Amblève set the stage for a showdown with Lieut. Colonel Peiper, the panzer leader whose SS troopers had run amuck near Malmédy. Peiper's task force still posed a threat on the northern flank, frightening civilians and Allies alike with assorted atrocities as it rolled, almost at will, down the Amblève River valley westward to the Meuse.

When Peiper left the Baugnez crossroads below Malmédy on the afternoon of December 17, his route lay south along the road to Ligneuville, a pretty resort town, where in happier times tourists had to come to hunt wild boar and deer in the forests nearby. The Germans hoped to capture an American command post said to be located there. But the Americans—an antiaircraft artillery unit—learned that a big panzer force was on its way, and most of them wisely

cleared out of their headquarters in the Hotel du Moulin minutes before it arrived.

The Germans did manage to capture a rear-guard force of 22 American soldiers—eight of whom were taken out and shot. The killings were witnessed by the Hotel du Moulin's amiable proprietor, Peter Rupp, an ardent Belgian patriot who had helped to smuggle out downed Allied airmen during the German Occupation. In a rage, the elderly Rupp flew at the executioner, an SS sergeant, shouting, "Murderer!" The sergeant hit Rupp, knocking out two of his teeth, and then an onlooking German officer muttered, "Shoot them all. The Belgian swine, too."

Rupp and the 14 Americans were being herded outside the inn when a second SS officer, higher in rank, intervened. In tones of contempt for his bloodthirsty comrades, he countermanded the execution order. Though grateful for his life, Rupp was still worried. The Germans were in a foul mood and might resume the killing at any moment. Then inspiration dawned: he descended quickly into his wine cellar and emerged with his arms full of bottles—his finest champagne and brandy. He passed the bottles out among the German troopers, and their mood quickly mellowed.

Pushing on from Ligneuville, Peiper's panzers met American tanks for the first time and, in a brisk fight, knocked out two Shermans and one M-10 tank destroyer, at a cost of one German Panther and two armored cars. After this encounter they advanced along a muddy, slippery forest road on the south bank of the winding Amblève River. At dusk on December 17 they reached the heights across from the village of Stavelot, and stopped to assess the situation.

The road curved sharply around a rocky cliff, then went straight across the river via a single stone bridge into the town, whose closely set buildings ominously resembled a fortress behind a moat. Peiper's forward scouts reported that the streets were full of trucks moving busily about with their headlights on. Although they were in fact only supply trucks assembling for a retreat, they gave the appearance of forces being massed for defense. But the panzers were running out of gas, and they had to plow forward in hopes of finding an American fuel dump.

Unknown to Peiper, a squad of the U.S. 291st Engineer Combat Battalion had set up a roadblock around the bend ahead, laying mines and backing them up with a bazoo-

U.S. vehicles, rushing fresh troops eastward to the defense of Saint-Vith on December 17, grind to a halt in a traffic jam many miles long. So great was the counterflow of retreating units that some reinforcements took half a day to cover the 12 miles from Vielsalm to Saint-Vith.

ka and a machine gun. Just ahead of the curve, Sergeant Charles Hensel had stationed a single man, Private Bernard Goldstein, as a lookout.

Peiper's lead tanks approached the curve slowly, as if feeling their way, the infantrymen on their decks talking to one another. Back at the roadblock, Hensel was astounded to hear Goldstein suddenly challenge the Germans with a loud, authoritative "Halt!" To Hensel it was wild, funny, magnificent: one GI, armed only with a rifle, commanding a whole German armored column to stop in its tracks.

The instant Goldstein spoke, the SS troopers leaped off their perches and opened fire; their shots were followed swiftly by the chatter of the tanks' machine guns and the boom of their cannon. The first shell went right over Goldstein's head, the muzzle blast momentarily blinding and deafening him. Stunned but alive, the private hightailed it up over the hill above the road. Peiper's panzers pressed on toward the Stavelot bridge. As the lead tank started around the bend, it was knocked out by Hensel's mines. Peiper, realizing that his vehicles could be picked off one by one on the narrow road, sent some 60 men on foot to try to take the bridge by storm, but they were quickly driven back.

Peiper stopped again to ponder his situation. A tank company sent down an alternate route returned with the news that the road was impassable. Meanwhile, most of his men had fallen asleep; they had had no rest for almost three days. Around midnight, a lieutenant from one of Skorzeny's commando units arrived from the rear with the news that Peiper's supporting units had bogged down in mud and were strung out for miles in a huge traffic jam. It was then, Peiper later said, that he began to sense that "the big strike was over." Bone-tired himself, he decided to close down for the night, wait until some support came up and then make his attack on Stavelot at dawn. The delay gave the Americans a few precious hours to boost their defenses.

That night, the defenders of Stavelot were reinforced by a company of an armored infantry battalion and a platoon of 3-inch antitank guns. The detachment's commander, Major Paul J. Solis, was getting his men and guns into position just before daybreak when the Germans attacked. Two Panther tanks charged around the curve and raced toward the bridge, which the Americans had unaccountably failed to destroy. Though the first Panther was hit and set afire on the bridge, it still had enough momentum to cross over and crash through a roadblock. Another tank shot the gap, followed by other vehicles and infantrymen, who drove the Americans back to the center of the town.

A probable reason why the bridge was not blown up emerged much later. At first it was thought that either the explosives or wiring placed on the span was defective. But months afterward, an engineer sergeant reported an intriguing encounter with a German prisoner in Le Havre. The prisoner hailed him in English, saying, "What outfit are you with?" When the sergeant told him, the German remarked with a laugh, "You were at Stavelot. I can tell you why that bridge wouldn't blow. We fixed it so it wouldn't." The German said no more, but the sergeant recalled that during the confusion of the night before the attack, with several different American units milling around, he had seen some unknown GIs loitering by the bridge. The prisoner's words convinced him that those mysterious men had been disguised members of a Skorzeny commando team and that they had sabotaged the engineers' effort to blow the bridge.

As Peiper's tanks and half-tracks poured across the river into Stavelot, they met fierce fire from the village square. Peiper ordered the bulk of his column to turn left through the outskirts of town and head for his next objective, Trois-Ponts, leaving a sizable detachment to deal with Stavelot.

Meanwhile, as Peiper's column headed west, his SS troopers in Stavelot ran amuck. On the edge of the woods near the Amblève bridge, they shot eight unarmed American prisoners of war. A German tank fired on eight Belgian civilians, killing two of them and severely wounding two others. Elsewhere, troops fired into a group of 20 civilians, killing three or four and wounding others. Later, the Germans discovered 26 Belgian civilians huddled in the basement of a house on the outskirts of the town. The soldiers hurled grenades into the cellar. Some of the Belgians survived the explosions and cried out that they were civilians; they were ordered out of the cellar and cut down by machine-pistol and rifle fire. Before the killing subsided in Stavelot, 101 people had been murdered.

After holding the marketplace at Stavelot for several hours, Major Solis and his troops, outnumbered and outgunned, retreated northward up a high, winding mountain road with

An American soldier in Stavelot gazes at the body of a child shot by the Germans. On recapturing the town from Joachim Peiper's panzers on the 19th of December, the GIs found 93 civilians—men, women and children—shot to death. Civilians told them that the children had been killed because their crying had annoyed the SS troopers.

the panzers in pursuit. A mile from Stavelot, Solis reached the edge of an enormous gasoline dump, where cans containing nearly two million gallons of fuel were stacked by the road for several miles. Only a handful of soldiers guarded the dump, and Solis had no heavy weapons left with which to defend it. Thinking quickly, he ordered his weary men to construct a roadblock of gasoline cans behind a bend in the steep road. They hastily flung hundreds of cans across the road, keeping up their work until they heard the angry growl of the panzers climbing through the tight curves toward them.

As the first German tank came in sight, the GI touched off the giant conflagration. The tank commander was stopped by the towering sheet of flames and could not detour through the thick woods on either side of the road. So he spun his tank around and headed back. The other tanks followed suit, retreating down the mountain. Later that day, a battalion of the 30th Infantry Division came down the

road to the relief of Stavelot, and took over the defense of the dump. Thanks to the ingenuity of Major Solis, Peiper had again been thwarted.

Yet another frustration for the Germans lay ahead in Trois-Ponts, where the Amblève and Salm Rivers joined. A company of American engineers had been rushed there to mine the town's bridges. Along the way, they had picked up some unexpected artillery—a 57mm antitank gun and its crewmen, separated from their unit. The engineers stationed the gun at the first and most important bridge, and hurriedly began attaching their explosives to the span. The gun crew waited like David for Goliath, their weapon little more than a slingshot against the big cannon of Panther and Tiger tanks.

Shortly before noon, with the engineers still at work, 19 German tanks approached Trois-Ponts. The lead panzer fired and missed. The 57mm crew quickly answered, disabling the tank by knocking off one of its treads. The

crewmen kept up their fire and held back the German column for 15 minutes—until the engineers had finished. The bridge blew up with a tremendous roar. Moments later, a German 88mm shell landed flush on the little gun, killing all four of its crewmen. For the panzer colonel, the loss of the bridge was a bitter blow. "If we had captured the bridge at Trois-Ponts intact," he said later, "and had had enough fuel, it would have been a simple matter to drive through to the Meuse River early that day."

With the main road to the west closed to him, Peiper turned his tanks northward and pressed on to the village of La Gleize to probe for an alternate route. He encountered little resistance around La Gleize, but after heading south again over a bridge at Cheneux, he ran into more bad luck. A tiny American observation plane, scudding along beneath low gray clouds, spotted the winding German column and called in a strike of fighter-bombers. Before the planes finally broke off the action because of thickening ground fog, Peiper had lost two more hours and 10 vehicles, including three tanks. Even more important, First Army headquar-

This vast American fuel dump—more than 400,000 five-gallon jerry cans of gasoline lining five miles of roadway between the Belgian towns of Stavelot and Francorchamps—lay just one mile from Joachim Peiper's gas-starved panzers after they crossed the Stavelot bridge on December 18. But American units retreating along the Francorchamps road turned back reconnoitering German tanks by setting up an immense flaming roadblock in which 124,000 gallons of fuel were consumed.

ters to the north at Spa now knew the precise location of the panzer force.

Peiper regrouped his scattered column and struck out for Werbomont, only four miles away. But as he approached the narrow Lienne Creek at the crossroads of Habiémont, more U.S. engineers were waiting for him. A squad under the command of Lieutenant Alvin Edelstein had just finished wiring the Habiémont bridge and was now engaged in blocking the feeder roads with mines.

Around 5 p.m., the engineers spotted the procession of German tanks—dark shadows passing behind the trees in the fading daylight. A Tiger fired its 88mm cannon at the Americans, but the shot was off target. Corporal Fred Chapin waited with the detonator in his hand until Lieutenant Edelstein screamed "Blow! Blow!" Then Chapin turned the key. To his immense relief, he saw the familiar string of blue flashes, followed by a thunderous blast.

As the machine guns of the lead tanks searched them out, the engineers ran up the road to a moving truck, leaped aboard and made good their escape. Peiper carried no heavy bridging equipment; it would have slowed down his fast-moving task force. He had no choice but to head back to La Gleize once more and try to find another route.

Retreating northward, Peiper seized La Gleize and the outlying towns of Cheneux and Stoumont and attempted to turn them into a fortified triangle. By then, however, he was boxed in by the 30th Infantry and 82nd Airborne Divisions; 10 miles to his rear, the bulk of the 1st SS Panzer Division was unable to get across the Amblève River at Stavelot, which had been recaptured by the 30th Division, or to cross the Salm River near Trois-Ponts. Peiper's spearhead had been cut off from the supplies of fuel, food and ammunition it so desperately needed.

The panzers fought fiercely for several days but were driven back into a pocket around La Gleize. By the afternoon of December 23, Peiper realized that his only hope was to try to break out to the east and get back to his lines.

As American artillery pounded the town, Peiper ordered his senior American prisoner, Major Hal D. McCown of the 30th Division, to be brought to his cellar command post. In a previous talk, McCown had found Peiper educated, fluent in English and not without a sense of humor. But McCown had heard the news of the Malmédy massacre and was worried about Peiper's 149 American prisoners. He had pointedly asked the panzer colonel his intentions. Peiper had smiled and explained that on the Russian front, where he had served, both Germans and Russians treated each other like beasts, but that on the Western Front the Germans fought under different rules.

Now, said Peiper, he would like to make a deal. In order to pull out and make it back to safety, he would have to abandon all vehicles and equipment, all wounded and prisoners of war. He proposed to free the American prisoners, holding only McCown as hostage, if McCown would guarantee that the American commander who took La Gleize would free all the German wounded. McCown replied that he had no authority to bind the American command to any agreement; all he could do was sign a statement that he had heard Peiper make the offer. The statement was written and signed and given to another American prisoner, a captain, to hold.

Around 1 o'clock the following morning, the remnants of Peiper's troops—some 800 men out of a force that originally numbered 5,000—left La Gleize silently and on foot. The troopers crossed a small bridge over the Amblève River and headed into the woods, hoping to filter through the 82nd Airborne's lines. For hours, McCown and Peiper trudged side by side through the darkness and the foot-deep snow. After daybreak cleared, Peiper pointed to a fir tree, sparkling brilliantly in the sun. "Major," he said with a sardonic smile, "the other night I promised you I would get you a tree for Christmas. There it is."

That night, Christmas Eve, the tired Germans ran into American outposts some three miles south of Trois-Ponts. In the fire fight that followed, McCown managed to slip off into the bushes. For a while he lay still, then started crawling in the direction of the American shooting. After covering about 100 yards, he stood up and walked cautiously forward, whistling a popular American tune as loud as he could. Then someone shouted out of the darkness, "Halt, goddamn it!" McCown knew he was home.

Peiper and his troopers were just as lucky. That night, they swam across the icy, roiling Salm River and made contact with German units four miles to the east. Behind them they left a trail of 353 prisoners of war and 111 civilians, killed in cold blood.

THE GI VS. WINTER

On guard duty in the frigid, snow-clad Ardennes, a lone GI of the 7th Armored Division patrols the shell-torn outskirts of Saint-Vith after its recapture in January.

NO ESCAPE FROM THE COLD AND SNOW

A dead German soldier, killed in an Ardennes ambush and frozen stiff with his arms outstretched, draws the pensive attention of an American trooper.

As his unit moved toward Bastogne in January 1945, Private Lester Atwell joined the GIs' struggle against an enemy as tough as the Germans: the Ardennes winter. "The weather remained bitter cold," wrote Atwell, "and snow fell unendingly." The infantrymen manned "snowy foxholes and stood guard and went on patrol day and night. Their chapped hands split open, their lips cracked, their feet froze. They had heavy colds, chilblains, pneumonia and dysentery; they became stiff and exhausted from prolonged exposure, but they could not be relieved."

The GIs owed much of their suffering to a woeful lack of supplies. In part because supply lines had been overtaxed by the race toward Germany, and also because the winter proved unusually harsh, the U.S. Army had failed to provide its soldiers with combat gear to match the season. Admitted General Omar Bradley, "I had deliberately bypassed shipments of winter clothing in favor of ammunition and gasoline. We had gambled in our choice, and now we were paying." In fact, large stocks of woolen clothing and waterproof boots did not begin arriving until mid-January—when the fighting was on the wane.

The first heavy snows had come late on December 21, and they actually helped some GIs. Mobile units that had bogged down on muddy roads suddenly made headway, with daredevil drivers skidding along in what they called "armored Frigidaires"—i.e., tanks. But the snow and frigid temperatures were torture for the foot soldiers: The men who broke trails through the drifts were worn out after struggling only 100 yards. The GIs' M-1 rifles sometimes froze, and a soldier caught in a sudden skirmish had only one way to free up his weapon: urinating on the rifle's moving parts. Wounded men beyond the reach of their buddies froze to death, their faces turning as red as claret.

In mundane but agonizing ways, the weather exacted a terrible toll. Trench foot and frostbite were epidemic; in the case of the 30th Division, they accounted for almost a third of the 1,390 casualties. Commented one GI ruefully, "All this damned fresh air is going to be the death of me."

A rifleman returns from the front lines wearing a sweater as a makeshift turban under his helmet. Some GIs cut leg holes in sleeping bags and wore them.

Breaking out of the fog, 3rd Armored Division troops storm a German-held village in the Ardennes.

Dangerously outlined against the snow, infantrymen of the 30th Division trudge toward Saint-Vith.

SNOW-BLIND AND FOGBOUND IN THE FOREST

Wind-driven snow, dense fogs and low-hanging clouds often reduced visibility in the Ardennes to 10 yards, so that, as a 2nd Infantry Division officer wrote, men materialized "like ghosts in the Belgian forest." Opposing patrols blinded by snow stumbled on each other in the fog, and on at least one occasion both sides fled in surprise without firing a single shot.

Even more perilous were the sudden and unpredictable breaks in the ground fog, which turned uncamouflaged soldiers into perfect targets against the white snow. To deny enemy marksmen such an advantage, the Americans launched most of their attacks under the cover of darkness.

Advancing from tree to tree, infantrymen offer

the enemy only brief targets. But the shielding trees turned deadly when hit by shellfire, showering men with branches and splinters as well as shell fragments.

Setting up a command post in a captured German hut, ebullient 5th Division infantrymen display a rare amenity—a chair.

An ingenious GI emerges

In a typical bivouac in the snow, soldiers of the 75th Infantry Division make do with shared blankets and pup tents.

from his improvised burrow to greet a medic. After digging a trench, the GI used the framework of an abandoned hay rake to support an elevated straw roof.

BATTLING FOR SHELTER, WARM FOOD AND A SHAVE

The GIs, desperate for shelter from the Ardennes cold, fought what they called the "Bitter Battle for Billets." In their attacks on German-held hamlets and farmhouses, they often risked their lives unnecessarily in close combat with rifle and bayonet rather than calling for artillery fire that might destroy potential barracks. But most of the time, the GIs had to bivouac in the snow, and so they learned to improvise with materials at hand.

For insulation against the frigid wind and frozen earth, the soldiers lined and roofed their foxholes with tenting cloth, straw or branches, and then threw their spare clothing on top. They also took advantage of body heat, with two or three men bedding down together.

To warm their food and feet, GIs exploited anything flammable: green pine branches, ration boxes or tin-can "desert stoves" containing a sooty, slow-burning mixture of sand and gasoline. One GI who craved a shave heated water in his steel helmet by placing it next to a truck's hot exhaust pipe. But many GIs found no relief from their suffering. Wrote a paratrooper of the 101st Airborne Division, "I cannot remember ever being warm."

129

As fellow members of a First Army artillery team congregate around a morning campfire, two men boldly strip to the waist in order to wash and shave.

A GI warms his feet and dries out his footwear at a scrap-wood fire. Some soldiers warmed up with the flammable tablets meant for heating their rations.

Exhausted foot soldiers of the 80th Division wolf down a lunch of cold rations and lukewarm coffee. They were among the lucky minority who had galoshes.

Blasting a foxhole with TNT, GIs are showered with chunks of frozen earth.

CARVING DEFENSES IN THE FROZEN EARTH

The instant that GIs came under enemy fire, they sprawled on their bellies in the snow and reflexively began digging in. But the ground was usually frozen solid a half foot deep, and it stubbornly resisted the GIs' standard entrenching equipment—a folding shovel and a short-handled pickax designed for use in the prone position. With bullets whining overhead, infantrymen sometimes hacked at the earth for hours just to get a narrow trench barely deep enough for their recumbent forms.

The only efficient way to break through the frozen crust was by using explosives. U.S. engineers provided a few fortunate units with small TNT charges that blasted through the rock-hard surface, exposing softer earth that soldiers could easily manage with their usual tools.

Chest-deep in a pit dug laboriously with shovels, members of an 81mm mortar

team fire on German positions near Saint-Vith. The Americans, advancing or retreating with the tide of battle, spent much of their time digging new positions.

A WOUNDED GI'S ODYSSEY

An American medic drags a wounded soldier—strapped to a stretcher set on runners—toward an aid station just behind a snowy battlefield in the Ardennes.

THE LONG CHAIN OF MEDICAL RESCUE

"Medic! Medic! I've been hit!" That cry was heard with horrifying frequency on the battlefields of the Ardennes, where nearly 47,500 American soldiers were wounded during six weeks of cruel winter fighting. Almost always, the U.S. Army's Medical Service came to the rescue in its own complex war against damage to flesh and bone.

The two or three aid men assigned to each rifle company were only the first link in the Medical Service's 4,500-mile-long chain of evacuation. The distance a wounded GI was passed along this route depended on how badly he was hit. A slightly injured man returned to duty from an aid station near the front line, while soldiers with grave wounds traveled farther and farther to the rear, through two more forward stations, a field hospital and an evacuation hospital to a general hospital. Eventually some wounded men were sent to hospitals in the U.S.

This chain, which had functioned smoothly throughout Europe up to December 1944, was suddenly disrupted by the Germans' counterattack in the Ardennes. The Medical Service found itself in what one doctor called "massive confusion. The U.S. Army had never told us anything about retreating." Frontline stations were overrun by Germans, and more than 247 staff members were killed or captured.

But order was soon brought out of chaos. The medics loaded transportable casualties on vehicles, left someone behind to care for the nontransportable and set up shop in the rear. They also arranged to aid units surrounded by the Germans. Containers of blood were placed in artillery shells and fired to the troops, supplies were delivered by parachute, and surgeons sped to the scene by glider. Recalled a sergeant in a surrounded unit, "The prettiest sight in the world were those docs gliding in."

By January 1, the Medical Service had expanded and strengthened its evacuation chain to handle the heavy influx of wounded. How the chain worked—how it ultimately saved 96 per cent of the 369,000 men wounded in the European theater—is shown here in a mosaic of photographs taken just before or during the Battle of the Bulge.

Huddling beside a makeshift stove, a medic shares the miseries of the Ardennes front line with the fighting men of a tank-destroyer battalion.

Under enemy fire, company aid men bandage an infantryman's shattered leg. In doing dangerous frontline work, more than 2,000 medics were killed in Europe.

Combat soldiers head for their aid station carrying a wounded buddy on a door covered with straw.

FIRST AID AT THE FRONT

During the hectic fighting in the Ardennes, company aid men were always on the run, bandaging wounds, giving morphine shots, administering sulfa and plasma. With temperatures hovering around 0°, medics carried their syringes in their armpits to keep the morphine from freezing as they darted from one casualty to another. In one day-long battle, an aid man treated so many wounded GIs that he later admitted: "I got sort of in a daze, putting on bandages, sticking the needle in."

The stretcher-bearers also pushed themselves to the brink of exhaustion, carrying the wounded through hip-deep snowdrifts and along icy roads. The danger of dropping wounded men prompted some medics to improvise sleds. They requisitioned skis from the townspeople and fitted them to stretchers, or fashioned runners from beams and strips of metal taken from damaged tin roofs.

Fortunately for the stretcher-bearers and the walking wounded, the battalion aid station was rarely more than 500 yards behind the front lines. Sometimes it was set up in a farmhouse kitchen, the cellar of a bombed-out building, or an abandoned barn; but in many cases, medical teams had to make do without shelter. "Wherever my jeep was," said a battalion surgeon who was attached to the 4th Armored Division, "that's where my station was."

In their crude clinic, the surgeon and technicians worked swiftly to give emergency treatment and ready badly wounded men for transport to the rear. They cleaned mud-caked wounds and dusted them with sulfa powder. They applied airtight bandages to sucking chest wounds, controlled hemorrhaging and set and splinted broken and torn limbs. The immediate treatment was limited, but its promptness saved the lives of thousands of GIs.

Medics set up a battalion aid station under the

cover of a thicket. To stay near the shifting front line, aid stations for the infantry sometimes moved daily; stations for armored units often moved almost hourly.

A battle casualty, sledded in on skis, is transferred to a jeep that has been rigged for carrying stretchers.

Bundled up in blankets, two disabled soldiers arrive at a field station in Belgium on a "weasel."

Medics unload an ambulance full of wounded GIs

TWO STOPOVERS BEHIND THE BATTLE LINE

About one mile behind the front line, a wounded man reached his next way station, or a regimental collecting point. It was only a short stopover. The doctors and a few technicians on duty checked the wounded for signs of hemorrhage or shock, gave them emergency treatment as needed, then sent them on by ambulance to the division's clearing station several miles farther to the rear.

At the clearing station, a team of doctors separated the incoming patients into three groups. Soldiers with minor wounds were treated and then returned to their units. The more serious casualties who were fit to travel were moved another 15 miles to an evacuation hospital. Men wounded so critically that they could not travel farther were rushed to the nearby field hospital for emergency treatment.

at a 5th Division clearing station in Luxembourg. En route to the rear, ambulances were frequently delayed by ice-covered roads, snowdrifts and enemy fire.

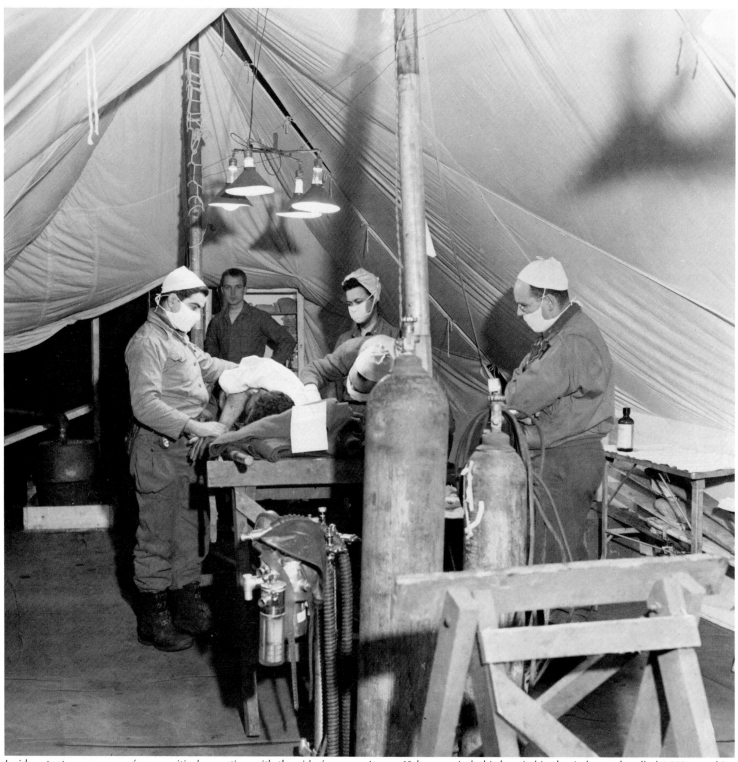

Inside a tent, surgeons perform a critical operation with the aid of a nurse. In one 63-hour period, this hospital in the Ardennes handled 1,000 casualties.

OPERATIONS IN TENTS, EVACUATION TO THE REAR

The standard field hospital was a collection of tents heated by potbellied stoves and equipped with beds for 300 patients. Here, men with serious wounds received lifesaving surgery and up to 12 days of postoperative care. But these hospitals had only limited equipment and staffs so small that traveling teams of surgeons had to be called in when casualties were heavy.

One doctor tersely explained the function of a field hospital by a reference to the many patients who arrived with mangled arms and hands: "We were not trying to get them ready to play a piano, we were just trying to get them to larger institutions for better care."

The next institution in a wounded combat soldier's journey was an evacuation hospital, some 15 miles farther to the rear. It was better equipped and could handle 400 to 750 patients at a time. Many soldiers returned to combat directly from the evacuation hospitals. Those soldiers requiring long convalescence or additional surgery were made ready for the long voyage out of the combat zone.

A Medical Service ambulance, hit by a German plane despite Red Cross markings, burns near a village in Luxembourg. The driver and patients perished.

Soldiers suffering from minor wounds or frostbite wait their turn for treatment in a busy evacuation hospital in Huy, Belgium, during the Battle of the Bulge.

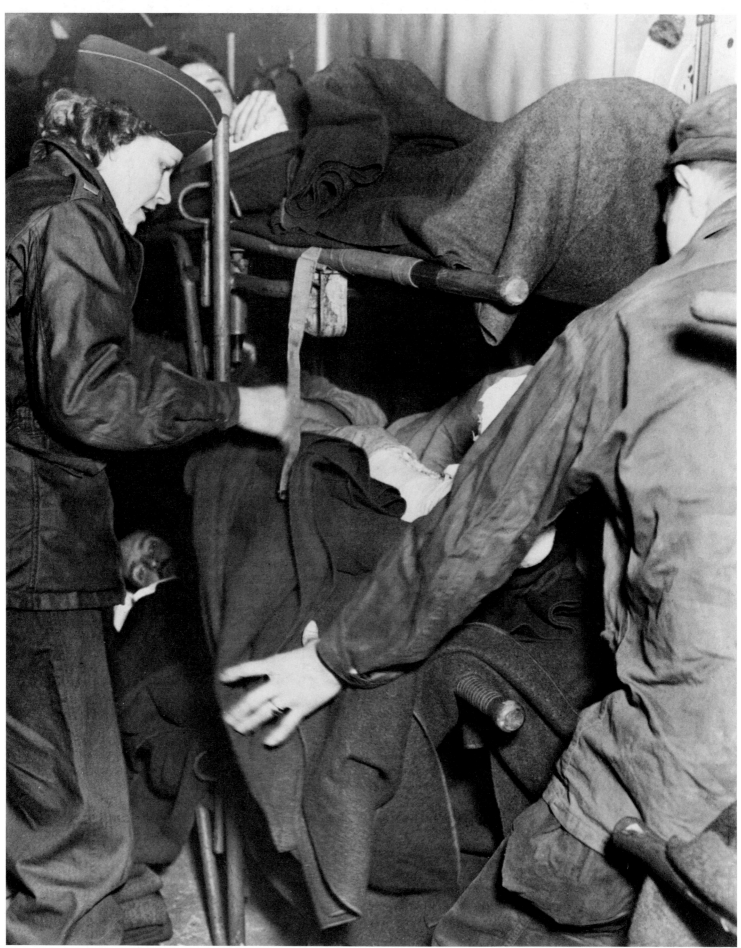

Aboard a hospital train, an Army nurse and a medic make patients comfortable for the trip to a hospital in the rear. Each train carried as many as 340 patients.

LAST STAGES OF THE JOURNEY

Soldiers who were badly wounded were evacuated from the combat zone in well-equipped hospital trains operated by the U.S. Transportation Corps and staffed by the Medical Service. Every train had its own pharmacy and an operating room to meet the medical needs of patients while they were en route to one of the 91 general hospitals scattered throughout western Belgium, Holland, France and England.

The general hospitals were often housed in such emergency quarters as military barracks or school buildings, but each had a staff of 125 doctors and nurses and 450 enlisted technicians to care for 1,000 patients. Here the most difficult operations were performed. However, some patients still needed corrective surgery and months of rehabilitation. To make room for incoming cases, these men were put on planes or hospital ships to "the Zone of the Interior": the United States.

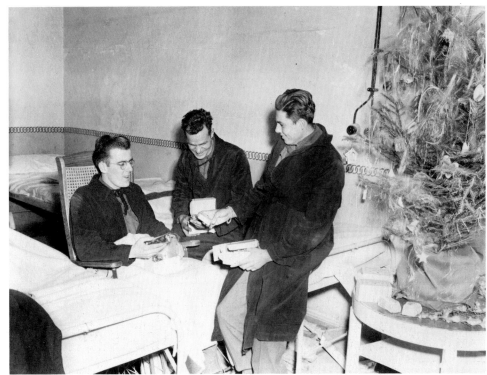

Soldiers, resting in a general hospital in Liège, open Christmas presents sent by the Red Cross.

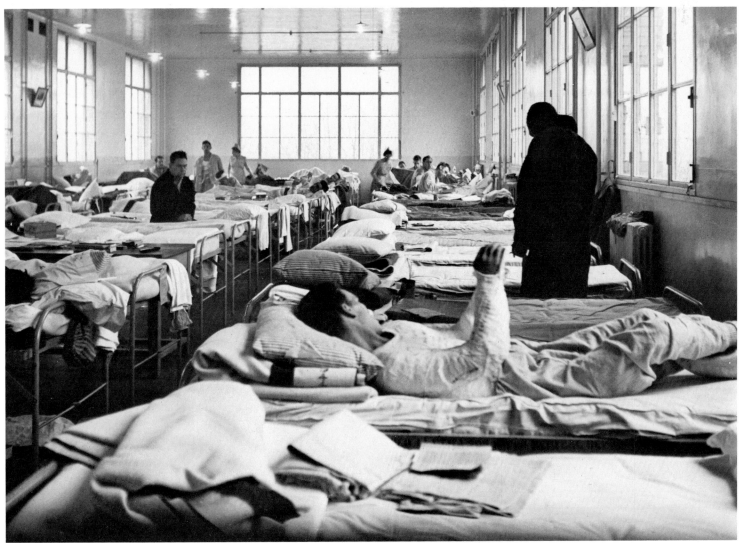

A GI with shell-torn arms waits in a general hospital in Paris for a flight to the U.S. Three days later, he was sent on the last stage of his journey (overleaf).

A cargo hoist lifts the wounded man into a C-54 bound for the U.S.

After landing at Mitchel Field on Long Island, the GI is wheeled to a waiting

ambulance. *The soldier stayed in a clinic at the airfield for a couple of weeks and then was sent to an Army hospital near his hometown in upstate New York.*

5

The paratroopers' mission: "Hold at all costs"
A nightmare of "tanks, tanks, tanks"
Plugging the gap with Team SNAFU
The sudden caution of a bold panzer general
A grisly clash at Noville
The 101st's great flapjack feast
General McAuliffe's famous last word
Supplies from the sky for Bastogne
A Christmas present from the Luftwaffe
Stopping the Germans a mile from victory
Private Hendrix' one-man war
Raising a toast in water

While the 7th Armored Division and other battered American units were desperately delaying Manteuffel's panzers around Saint-Vith, the biggest and longest fight in the Battle of the Bulge was shaping up at Bastogne, some 30 miles to the southwest. Bastogne, a drab market town of 3,500 inhabitants, was fated to be a battlefield because of the seven paved roads that radiated in all directions from its central square. These roads included the main east-west highways running from the German border to Dinant and the Meuse River—vital routes in Hitler's thrust toward Antwerp.

The commanders on both sides were acutely aware of Bastogne's importance. Manteuffel knew that his main force —the three divisions of the 47th Corps and their supporting truck convoys—needed those roads for swift passage through the Ardennes's jumbled, wooded terrain. Hitler himself considered Bastogne to be indispensable and had made it an exception to his rule that the panzer units should bypass towns and leave the assault work to the infantry. The Führer had given Manteuffel permission to attack Bastogne with his panzers if he met with unexpectedly heavy resistance there.

In the American camp, General Eisenhower too realized the importance of Bastogne to the defense of the Ardennes; as early as December 17, he and his commanders alerted three divisions—the 10th Armored and the 82nd and 101st Airborne—for movement to the general area.

The 101st Airborne, nicknamed "the Screaming Eagles" after the fierce bird on its shoulder patch, had suffered one-third casualties in Field Marshal Montgomery's abortive airborne attack in Holland, and had recently been stationed around the French town of Mourmelon-le-Grand, 20 miles southeast of Rheims and nearly 100 miles southwest of Bastogne, for resupply, replacement of casualties and re-training. It seemed so unlikely that the 101st would be called on to fight again soon that officials of the U.S. War Department had summoned the division's commanding officer, Major General Maxwell D. Taylor, back to Washington to attend a conference.

On the night of December 17, a dozen or so officers of the 101st Airborne were enjoying a housewarming party in the old French military post at Mourmelon-le-Grand. The hosts were the division's intelligence officer, Lieut. Colonel Paul A. Danahy, and his close friend Lieut. Colonel Harry

THE SIEGE OF BASTOGNE

W. O. Kinnard, the operations officer. They had engaged a French chef to cook a fine meal, had rounded up an ample supply of gin, champagne and brandy, and had borrowed a movie projector to show an old Gary Cooper film.

The after-dinner drinks were being sipped and the movie unreeled when the party suddenly came to an end: Brigadier General Anthony C. McAuliffe, acting commander of the 101st in General Taylor's absence, had summoned staff and regimental officers to an emergency meeting. McAuliffe came right to the point in his quiet, undramatic manner. He explained that the 101st had been ordered to the Belgian town of Werbomont and was to move out early the next morning. "All I know," he said, "is that there has been a breakthrough, and we have got to get up there."

Feverish preparations began at once, and trucks were called in from as far away as Paris and Rouen to make up a convoy of 380 vehicles. The division's 11,000 men started moving out in combat teams at 9 a.m. on the 18th; the last batch did not get under way until 8 p.m. The groups took about eight hours to complete their cold, dreary, bone-jarring ride north.

General McAuliffe and Lieut. Colonel Kinnard sped into the Ardennes well ahead of the troops. As their command car approached a crossroads about 30 miles from Werbomont, McAuliffe decided to detour to General Middleton's VIII Corps headquarters in Bastogne to find out what was going on. The road outside Bastogne was clogged with troops heading west, away from the front, and McAuliffe was more than a little concerned by the time he reached Middleton's headquarters in a brick barracks on the northwestern edge of town.

By way of greeting, Middleton informed the visitors in his soft Mississippi drawl: "There has been a major penetration. Certain of my units, especially the 106th and 28th Divisions, are broken." Many German units were bearing down on Bastogne. Middleton's situation map, with U.S. troops conventionally represented in blue and enemy units in red, looked to one officer as though it was suffering from a bad case of measles.

The upshot, Middleton explained, was that his headquarters was being withdrawn to Neufchâteau, 18 miles to the southwest, and that McAuliffe's orders had been changed. Instead of going northwest to Werbomont, the 101st Airborne was to take over the defense of Bastogne—and to hold it at all costs.

McAuliffe had visions of the Germans bursting into Bastogne before he could organize and deploy the 101st. He jumped into his staff car and headed back toward the junction of the Werbomont road. Four miles west of town he came upon Mande-Saint Etienne, one of many farming villages that ringed Bastogne, and he chose it as a bivouac and staging area. He issued orders that his four regiments be headed off and directed there.

Meanwhile, back at VIII Corps headquarters, Middleton received another welcome arrival, his old friend Colonel William L. Roberts, whose Combat Command B of the 10th Armored Division was rushing toward Bastogne from France. Middleton went to the map and indicated the three German columns that were converging on Bastogne on the three main roads leading west into the town square. He said he needed three combat teams, one each to guard the three roads at junctions four to six miles east of Bastogne.

"That's no way to use armor," objected Roberts, mindful of the textbook dictum that tank units should be wielded en masse to slug the enemy with concentrated force.

"Robbie, I may not know as much about the employment of armor as you, but that's the way I have to use them."

Roberts immediately told the general that his Combat Command B could do the job.

"Move with utmost speed," Middleton ordered. "And Robbie, hold these positions at all costs."

As the tanks and troops of Combat Command B arrived in Bastogne, Roberts split them into three teams. First, he ordered Lieut. Colonel James O'Hara to take 500 men and 30 tanks and block the road from the southeast that led to Bastogne from the town of Wiltz. Lieut. Colonel Henry T. Cherry was packed off with a similar force toward Longvilly, directly east of Bastogne, to beef up the remnants of a combat team of the 9th Armored Division, which was already manning a roadblock there. Roberts told Major William R. Desobry to take the third task force to the northeast and to hold the town of Noville. As it happened, Noville stood directly in the path of the crack German 2nd Panzer Division and would see some of the fiercest fighting in the battle for Bastogne.

Desobry was just 26 years old, and Roberts, putting an

arm around the major's shoulders, offered him some fatherly advice. "By tomorrow morning," he said, "you'll probably be nervous. Then you'll probably want to pull out. When you begin thinking like that, remember I told you *not* to pull out."

The three combat teams moved out briskly to set up their shield around Bastogne. On the way, they met a steady stream of dazed, exhausted GIs—stragglers from a dozen units that had defended Clervaux, Wiltz and other towns to the east. The survivors recounted a litany of disaster, summed up by one muddy soldier as "tanks, tanks, tanks." The battered GIs trudged wearily into Bastogne, and some of them kept right on going to the rear. But others stayed to fight. Colonel Roberts rounded up as many as he could and organized them into a makeshift unit that would plug many a gap in Bastogne's defense perimeter in the days ahead. With heavy GI sarcasm, the stragglers christened their ragtag outfit Team SNAFU, from an Army word whose letters stood, approximately, for Situation Normal, All Fouled Up.

By late evening of the 18th, the lead trucks of the 101st Airborne began pulling into the division's assembly area at Mande-Saint Etienne. First to arrive was the 501st Parachute Infantry Regiment. As the 2,300 paratroopers climbed half-frozen from the open trucks and began setting up camp, their commanding officer reported to General McAuliffe at his Bastogne headquarters. The regimental commander was Lieut. Colonel Julian J. Ewell, a rail-thin West Point graduate. A veteran of the airdrops into Normandy and Holland, Ewell was highly regarded for his coolness under fire, his keen judgment of terrain and his lively sense of humor.

McAuliffe decided to send Ewell and his 501st Regiment to the east of Bastogne to reinforce Team Cherry, one of the three stopgap groups formed from Combat Command B of the 10th Armored. Pointing to the route to Longvilly on the map, McAuliffe said, "Move out along this road to the east at six o'clock, make contact with the enemy, attack and clear up the situation." Ewell replied, "Yes, sir," saluted and left. Returning to his regiment to organize for the 6 a.m. advance, Ewell encountered the regimental chaplain, who asked what was going on. "Father," said Ewell, "if I knew more, I'd be confused."

Though neither Ewell nor McAuliffe realized it at the time, the general had sent the lieutenant colonel to attack one of Manteuffel's two powerful armored divisions. Forward elements of the formidable Panzer Lehr Division, led by Major General Fritz Bayerlein, had reached the village of Niederwampach, a scant six miles east of Bastogne. In fact, Bayerlein's tanks might well have burst past Team Cherry and driven right into Bastogne's town square before Ewell's men could move. But two pieces of misinformation delayed Bayerlein's advance.

In Niederwampach, some civilians told Bayerlein that an unpaved shortcut from their village to the nearby hamlet of Mageret was passable for his tanks. In Mageret, they said, he could pick up the main route running from Longvilly into Bastogne. Eager to conquer his prize that night, the general led an advance guard of 15 Mark IV tanks down the unpaved road—only to discover that it soon deteriorated into a trough of mud. His heavy tanks spent four hours churning their way to Mageret, a distance of less than three miles.

There Bayerlein was misled again, this time by a Belgian who told him that a large force of some 50 American tanks and perhaps 75 other vehicles, commanded by a major general, had passed through Mageret about midnight, heading east. What the Belgian had actually seen was a portion of the far smaller Team Cherry. The report worried Bayerlein. He knew that U.S. major generals commanded at least a division, and he imagined that his planned advance might put him in position to be cut off by a large enemy armored force. The usually aggressive Bayerlein turned cautious. He halted in Mageret, set up roadblocks, planted a minefield and buttoned up for the night.

The next morning, December 19, Bayerlein started to move westward toward Bastogne. But as he reached the next little village of Neffe, a mile down the road from Mageret, his lead tank hit a mine and was disabled. Again Bayerlein paused. While his men cleared the roads of mines, Lieut. Colonel Ewell's regiment was heading in his direction, supported by the 101st Airborne Division's artillery.

Ewell was being careful, too. He sent the 1st Battalion, about 700 strong, to reconnoiter the road to Longvilly at 6 a.m. He told its commander, "Take it slow and easy—I don't want you to beat the enemy to death."

Ewell's caution paid off. When the 1st Battalion reached the outskirts of Neffe, it ran into what seemed to be a

German roadblock. Hearing machine-gun fire, Ewell raced in a jeep to the head of the column. He realized that his men had run into no mere roadblock; in fact, though no one yet realized it, they had encountered the vanguard of the Panzer Lehr. A head-on attack was out of the question.

Ewell told the 1st Battalion to hold its ground and then brought forward his 2nd and 3rd Battalions. One he placed on high ground to the north near a village called Bizory; the other he deployed on his southern flank. Having formed a solid front, Ewell called upon the divisional artillery back in

American antiaircraft gunners watch a high-speed dogfight between German interceptors and U.S. fighter-bombers flying escort for cargo planes bound for Bastogne. The gunners, afraid of hitting American planes by accident, held their fire and enjoyed the spectacle. The swirling pattern of vapor trails, remarked one soldier, "looked right pretty."

151

Bastogne to hit the German positions. The division's special light 105mm howitzers, usually carried aboard gliders during airborne assaults, zeroed in on the German forward positions and began a steady, killing fire.

Bayerlein's ruination was completed by his first encounter with Ewell's men at Neffe. The winter fog was so thick that he could not see what was going on, and the heavy shelling confirmed his suspicion that he faced a large force. He was so badly shaken that he went off to a cave near the Neffe railroad station to set up a command post and analyze the situation. As a result, the Panzer Lehr spent the whole day probing at one American outpost after another, but it failed to make a concerted drive on Bastogne.

Nevertheless, Bayerlein's panzers managed to do considerable damage to the U.S. forces east of the town. The night before, when Bayerlein had taken the long shortcut to Mageret, some of the tanks had infiltrated behind the American roadblock at Longvilly, imperiling the two defending units there, the task force from the 9th Armored Division and the advance section of Team Cherry. As these two groups tried to fight their way back through the German positions, their tanks and trucks bogged down in a traffic jam on the road from Longvilly to Bastogne. Panzer units spent the late afternoon shooting up the retreating American armor.

Lieut. Colonel Cherry, who found himself cut off from the main body of his task force, came under heavy fire in the command post in a stone château south of Neffe. The roof of the château was set afire by German shells, and Cherry and his staff were forced to pull back. "We're not driven out," Cherry radioed to his headquarters just before he reluctantly departed. "We were burned out. We're not withdrawing, we're moving."

Despite these reverses, General McAuliffe's first move had worked out well. Ewell's paratroopers, sent to bolster Team Cherry, had stood firm with most of the armored task force, preventing the German probes from making a breakthrough from the east. The defense of Bastogne had survived its first crisis.

While this thrust-and-parry engagement was being fought, another serious threat developed around the village of Noville, six miles to the northeast of Bastogne. Young Major Desobry, leading a team of 15 Sherman tanks, a platoon of tank destroyers and a company of armored infantry, arrived in the dreary, treeless village at about 11 p.m. on December 18. Desobry learned from GIs retreating through Noville that a large armored force—actually the entire 2nd Panzer Division—was hot on their heels. He posted roadblocks on the roads north and east of Noville and got set for battle.

He did not have to wait long. Before dawn, German tanks hit two of his roadblocks. Desobry's men beat back the attacks, then at 7:30 they followed his order to fall back to Noville. A heavy fog had settled in, blanketing the village and the surrounding fields, but the nervous defenders of Noville could hear the rumbling and clanking of German tanks in front of their defense perimeter. When the fog lifted at 10 a.m., they saw to their horror that the countryside to the north and east was crawling with German Tigers and Panthers; 30 tanks could be seen nearby and a dozen more were ranged on distant ridges.

Desobry's men threw at the Germans everything they had—bazooka rockets, .50-caliber machine-gun fire, antitank rounds. To the north, 14 German tanks hurried along an exposed ridge and 10 of them were picked off, one by one, by Desobry's few but powerful 90mm tank destroyers. Not a single panzer was able to get within 200 yards of the U.S. positions.

Frustrated, the Germans let loose with their artillery. Explosive shells rained on the exposed village, killing and wounding defenders, setting fires and leveling houses. Despite Colonel Roberts' warning the night before, Desobry

The only newspaper reporter in Bastogne during the siege, Fred MacKenzie of the Buffalo Evening News sits grimacing in a corner as he recuperates from a brush with death. MacKenzie stayed up late one night to type his notes in a room across the hall from his sleeping quarters. While he was working there, a German artillery shell scored a direct hit on his bunk, and the blast killed four GIs who were in the room.

began thinking it was high time to pull out of Noville. He radioed Roberts for permission to fall back to the village of Foy, on higher ground a mile nearer Bastogne.

Roberts told Desobry to use his own judgment, but informed him reinforcements were coming. Desobry decided to hang on. Colonel Robert F. Sink's 506th Parachute Infantry Regiment had meanwhile arrived in Bastogne, and Roberts rushed one battalion to Noville under Lieut. Colonel James L. LaPrade. Desobry and LaPrade launched a counterattack against the 2nd Panzer Division. But their remaining 13 medium tanks and about 1,000 troops made little headway against the Germans on the ridges that overlooked Noville. The Americans advanced only 500 yards before being pinned down.

At that juncture, the Germans launched an attack of their own. The paratroopers and tankmen managed to stop the assault at the edge of Noville, taking and inflicting heavy casualties. But the German bombardment continued. An 88mm shell burst just outside the American command post, killing LaPrade and seriously wounding Desobry.

All night long the GIs endured the shelling, and at first light on December 20 the panzers resumed the struggle. Just after daybreak two German tanks barreled into Noville. A bazooka team stopped one, and an American tank accounted for the other.

The panzers kept up their pressure on Noville through the morning, and the Americans kept fighting and dying. Finally, around noon, the survivors were ordered to fall back on Foy, which was now strongly held by the rest of Colonel Sink's regiment. In Noville, the wounded were loaded aboard half-tracks. Paratroopers climbed on every vehicle that was still functioning. Engineers blew up an ammunition dump and, as the fog closed in again, the column set off down the road, with an armored car, four half-tracks and five tanks in the lead.

About 500 yards from Foy the lead half-track halted; the second half-track rammed into it, and a wild melee ensued. Some Germans who had infiltrated behind Noville opened up with rifles and grenades. A hail of American machine-gun and rifle fire silenced them.

The column had no sooner lurched forward again than it was fired on by German tanks. Two of the five American tanks were disabled. A third broke down, and a fourth got away toward Bastogne but was hit as it reached Foy. The driver of the remaining tank climbed from the turret and went forward to try to help untangle the traffic jam, but he was hit. Now the road was blocked and the remaining tank was driverless. Paratroopers stormed up and down the column, shouting for a volunteer driver and calling the men in the 10th Armored task force "yellow bastards" when none came forward. But the task force included many replacements from other outfits—cooks, mechanics and riflemen—and none of them knew how to drive a tank. Disgusted, several paratroopers climbed aboard the driverless Sherman. "We'll learn how to drive the son of a bitch," one said. The tank roared to life, and the column took off cross-country toward Foy. By dusk the survivors had made their way back into the American lines.

The fight at Noville had been one of the grisliest small-scale clashes of the War. A GI whose unit later passed through the village said, "We found all manner of horrors. Stuff like a galosh with a foot still in it, a headless paratrooper, a blackened tree stump which turned out to be a cremated Kraut sitting in a foxhole, a paratrooper's helmet full of brains and meltwater, a severed arm with a wristwatch on it— all that sort of mincing-machine warfare."

Yet the grim defense put up by Team Desobry and La-Prade's battalion had delayed the powerful 2nd Panzer for almost 48 hours, destroying at least 20 of its tanks and the equivalent of half a regiment of panzer grenadiers. When the commander of the 2nd Panzer at last entered Noville and radioed his headquarters for permission to attack south-

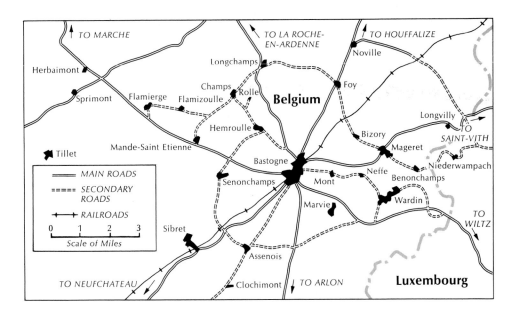

Bastogne, the principal crossroads town in the central Ardennes, controlled seven all-weather highways, a major railway and a network of secondary roads to surrounding villages. In American hands, Bastogne was a critical bottleneck for three German divisions, whose tanks, troops and supply convoys needed the roads to speed westward, avoiding arduous travel on unpaved secondary roads.

153

ward into Bastogne, an angry staff officer spat back, "Forget Bastogne and head for the Meuse." The High Command had decided that the task of capturing Bastogne would be left to Bayerlein's Panzer Lehr and Brigadier General Heinz Kokott's 26th Volksgrenadier Division.

By December 20, General McAuliffe was playing with a full hand. The entire 101st Airborne was now on the scene, along with all of Colonel Roberts' Combat Command B of the 10th Armored. In addition, the 705th Tank Destroyer Battalion—a crack outfit armed with new high-velocity 76mm guns—had arrived from the north.

With McAuliffe's approval, operations chief Kinnard had deployed these forces in a defensive arc around the town. He kept Ewell's regiment in place east of Bastogne along with Team Cherry. He also left Sink's regiment where it was, northeast of town in the neighborhood of Foy. Covering the northern perimeter, to the left of Sink's men, was the 502nd Parachute Infantry Regiment, commanded by Lieut. Colonel Steve A. Chappuis. South of Bastogne, Kinnard ranged a battalion of the 327th Glider Infantry Regiment, under Colonel Joseph H. "Bud" Harper. In the center, Kinnard stationed the artillery—seven battalions strong, including three battalions of long-range howitzers. The artillery could lob shells far enough to reach German forces anywhere along the defense perimeter.

That day the new defense line was tested at two spots. A strong thrust was aimed at the 10th Armored task force headed by Lieut. Colonel O'Hara, which was manning a roadblock near the town of Marvie, southeast of Bastogne. After shelling Team O'Hara, the Panzer Lehr sent in four tanks and six half-tracks full of panzer grenadiers. The half-tracks burst past O'Hara's roadblock and swept into Marvie. At this point, some of Colonel Harper's glider infantry entered the fight, engaging the Germans at hand-grenade range. The attackers blasted the glider troops with machine guns, leaped from their half-tracks and darted into Marvie's houses. Fighting raged for two hours before the glidermen managed to root out the panzer grenadiers.

At the same time, the Germans tried again to penetrate Lieut. Colonel Ewell's line east of Bastogne. Ewell's paratroopers watched an entire battalion of gray-clad infantrymen approach the northern end of their line near the village of Bizory, backed by two tanks and a pair of self-propelled guns. Nearby, the crews of four antitank guns soon spotted six more tanks.

Ewell's men began spraying the attacking soldiers with small-arms fire, and the antitank guns began firing at the oncoming tanks. One antitank gun was destroyed by a German shell, but the others battered the panzers. With their armored support backing off, the German infantrymen slowed their attack, seeking cover. At this point, McAuliffe tried out his centrally located artillery. Ewell's paratroopers near Bizory heard the "outgoing mail" whine overhead and saw the shells bursting among the German infantrymen. The barrage continued for 20 minutes, chopping the enemy attack to bits. After the artillery fire ended, Harry Kinnard relayed an unmilitary but heartfelt message from Ewell to McAuliffe: "Julian says you took care of the sonsabitches real, real good." McAuliffe and his staff enjoyed their first laugh since the division left Mourmelon-le-Grand.

Despite the heavy loss of Volksgrenadiers, the Germans returned to the attack on Ewell's front at 7 p.m. on the 20th. German artillery hit the road junctions east of Bastogne. When the firing let up, panzers and infantry attacked in the dark along the road from Neffe into Bastogne. McAuliffe's artillery shelled the terrain being crossed by the enemy, forming a wall of fire west of Neffe. Three German tanks were destroyed. Some infantrymen got past the exploding shells only to be driven away by the machine-gun fire of Ewell's 1st Battalion.

At almost the same time, other German infantry units attacked Ewell's right flank to the south. In the darkness the Americans could hear the enemy troops moving about. Firing at the sounds, the paratroopers could tell from the screams of the wounded that their random bullets were finding targets. But it was not until first light that the defenders realized exactly what had happened. The Germans had been charging across a field crisscrossed with farmers' wire fences. They had run into the wire and were struggling to free themselves when the American bullets killed them. Their bodies hung there in long gray windrows.

Despite the American successes early on December 20, McAuliffe decided that afternoon that the time had come to reassess the situation with General Middleton. He trusted the courage of his Screaming Eagles, but he was not willing to sacrifice more men on his own authority alone.

Late that day, a jeep sped McAuliffe southwest down the corridor that connected Bastogne with VIII Corps headquarters at Neufchâteau. McAuliffe told Middleton that he was confident Bastogne could be held for another two days and perhaps longer. Middleton replied that another enemy division—the 116th Panzer—was reported to be heading in his direction, and suggested that it might be best if the 101st were to pull out after all. "Hell," McAuliffe retorted, using his strongest expletive, "if we pull out now we'd be chewed to pieces." That was what Middleton had hoped to hear. "Good luck, Tony," he said with a grin. "Now don't get yourself surrounded."

McAuliffe raced back to Bastogne. As he reached his lines in the darkness, the road was cut behind him by German units circling the town to the north and south. Middleton's advice notwithstanding, the Americans were now surrounded—trapped in a lumpy circle some five miles in diameter.

That evening, Lieut. Colonel Kinnard took a call from General Ridgway's XVIII Airborne Corps headquarters, asking how things were going in Bastogne. Kinnard was reluctant to answer, realizing that the Germans were monitoring American radio transmissions. But when Ridgway's people insisted on a reply, Kinnard framed a guarded answer. "Visualize the hole in a doughnut," he said. "That's us."

The encirclement of Bastogne was followed by a lull in the fighting that lasted for two and a half days; the Germans were consolidating their positions and massing units for new attacks on the perimeter. The lull was welcome to the men of the 101st—and they did not mind being surrounded; airborne divisions were accustomed to dropping behind enemy lines and holding out until relief forces could break through. Harry Kinnard said with satisfaction that Bastogne was a "textbook situation" for the 101st.

What did worry the men was lack of supplies. Artillery shells were so short that McAuliffe ordered them severely rationed. To a protesting officer he said, tongue in cheek, "If you see four hundred Germans in a hundred-yard area, and they have their heads up, you can fire artillery at them. But not more than two rounds." Rifle ammunition was low as well. And the food supply was dwindling fast—except for tons of flour that had been found in a Bastogne granary. The flour made good flapjacks, and the men ate flapjacks until they were sick of them.

Medical facilities were dangerously skimpy. The 101st Airborne's medical unit, including most of its surgeons and equipment, had been captured by a roving German force on December 19, and the wounded were being cared for in a makeshift clinic, nursed by a few doctors and medical corpsmen and some Belgian civilian volunteers. Virtually the only painkiller on hand was brandy. Fortunately, it was in generous supply.

On December 22, General McAuliffe received some encouraging news: The 4th Armored Division, part of Patton's Third Army, was beginning its final drive north to relieve Bastogne, as ordered by General Eisenhower on the 19th. Patton had kept his vow to move three divisions—the 4th Armored, along with the 26th and 80th Infantry Divisions—out of the line in the Saar and get them into action on another front in less than 72 hours.

That day at about 11:30 a.m., Sergeant Oswald Y. Butler of the glider regiment spotted a group of Germans walking up the road from the town of Arlon toward the farmhouse he was occupying on the southern rim of the American perimeter. Butler quickly got on the field telephone to his command post. "There're four Krauts coming up the road," he reported. "They're carrying a white flag. It looks like they want to surrender."

The Germans—a major, a captain and a pair of enlisted men—carried a document and asked to be taken to the American commanding general. The envoys were ushered to the platoon command post, where the enlisted men were left under guard. The two German officers were then blindfolded and led to the company command post. They were held there while Major Alvin Jones carried their document to division headquarters. The rumor raced along the regiment's front: The Germans wanted to throw in the towel and had sent a party to arrange terms. Tired GIs clambered out of foxholes, chatted with their neighbors, built warming fires and even found time to shave for the event.

But when Major Jones arrived at division headquarters, he made it quite clear that the Germans had expressed no intention of surrendering. "It's an ultimatum, sir," Jones said to Lieut. Colonel Ned D. Moore, the 101st chief of staff. Moore took the two sheets of typewritten paper and

Wearing snowsuits hastily manufactured in Holland and western Belgium, Americans of the 7th Armored Division take the offensive in late January, 1945.

DRESSING IN WHITE FOR WINTER WARFARE

At dusk on December 23, 1944, German soldiers in white outer clothing advanced stealthily toward the American-held village of Marvie, southeast of Bastogne. In their white attire the attackers blended in perfectly with the snow-covered landscape, and they had proceeded all the way to the outskirts of Marvie before the defending troops of the 101st Airborne Division noticed the vague white figures and identified them as Germans. By then it was too late to stop the attack. The surprise effect, as one of the paratroopers remarked, "was terrific."

American artillerymen defending the southern Ardennes in Luxembourg pitch white tents that will help camouflage their campsite in a snowy field.

Crewmen of a U.S. armored battalion paint their M-4 tank white after a heavy snowfall.

GIs stand guard behind a camouflaged machine gun.

There was nothing new about winter camouflage. By 1942, snowsuits were issued to many German units as standard equipment, and the Allies had also used winter camouflage in several campaigns. But the Germans' unexpected and large-scale use of the white camouflage in the Ardennes afforded them an important—if temporary—edge.

At Bastogne and elsewhere, the Americans quickly came up with snowsuits of their own. Some GIs cadged bed sheets from civilians and made capes by cutting a hole in the center for the head. Others put on their white long johns over their standard combat clothing. Soon, proper winter camouflage uniforms started to flow to the front lines, and the protective white coloration was applied to a wide variety of other equipment, ranging from tanks to tents.

looked at them. "What does it say?" McAuliffe demanded.

"They want you to surrender," Moore replied.

The ultimatum said in part:

To the U.S.A. Commander of the encircled town of Bastogne:

The fortune of war is changing. This time the U.S.A. forces in and near Bastogne have been encircled by strong German armored units.

There is only one possibility to save the encircled troops from total annihilation: that is the honorable surrender of the encircled town.

McAuliffe looked briefly at the message. "Aw, nuts!" he said. Then he dropped the papers on the floor and strode out of the room.

When McAuliffe was reminded that the German emissaries were still waiting for a reply, he was stumped. "Well," he said, "I don't know what to tell them."

Lieut. Colonel Kinnard replied, "That first crack you made would be hard to beat, General."

"What was that?" McAuliffe asked.

"You said 'Nuts!'"

McAuliffe snapped his fingers, exclaiming: "That's it!"

Everyone in the room burst into laughter and a sergeant typed up the answer on a sheet of 8-by-11-inch bond:

To the German Commander:
Nuts!
The American Commander

McAuliffe gleefully handed his one-word reply to Colonel Harper, who had just arrived, and asked, "Will you see that it's delivered?"

The colonel glanced at the message and beamed. "I'll deliver it myself!"

Harper returned to the company command post where the German officers had been waiting. Handing McAuliffe's message to the major, he said, "If you don't understand what 'Nuts' means, in plain English it is the same as 'Go to hell.' And I will tell you something else—if you continue to attack, we will kill every goddamn German that tries to break into this city!"

The German major and captain saluted formally. "We will kill many Americans," the captain declared. "This is war."

"On your way, bud!" growled Harper. Then he added impulsively, "And good luck to you." As the little German party receded in the distance, Harper wondered what had come over him to make him wish his enemies good luck.

On December 23 the damp and foggy weather suddenly broke; the day dawned bright, clear and very cold. If the 10° temperature turned sodden boots to icy slabs and made flesh cling painfully to gun metal, it also provided fine flying weather for the first time in days, and the men of Bastogne received word that an airdrop was in the works. As the morning wore on, all eyes searched the blue skies for dark specks. At 9 o'clock, a pathfinder team parachuted in to set up its colored ground panels and radar to guide the incoming planes. A few minutes before noon, the first of 241 C-47 cargo carriers droned over the drop zone. Red, blue and yellow parachutes billowed like fantastic Christmas ornaments, floating downward with priceless gifts of ammunition, medical supplies and food. Not all of the planes made it; some, hit by flak as they flew over the German lines, wobbled along, trailing smoke as their pilots tried desperately to deliver their loads before their craft broke into flames and fell.

The exhilarated men of Bastogne rushed out to drag the heavy parapacks back through the snow. They discovered a few foul-ups, including some shells for guns they did not have. But nobody complained. More than 95 per cent of the 144 tons of matériel in 1,446 packages was recovered and put to use. "That's close enough for government work," Lieut. Colonel Kinnard cracked. As an added dividend, the 82 Thunderbolt fighter-bombers that had convoyed the cargo planes to Bastogne turned to hammer the German ring around the town, flashing in low with napalm, fragmentation bombs and machine-gun fire.

Though the cold snap had made it possible to supply Bastogne by air, it also helped the Germans. Now that the ground was frozen, their tanks and half-tracks were able to maneuver across previously muddy terrain. Manteuffel had sent the 2nd Panzer Division past Bastogne toward the Meuse, but he was still determined to capture the surrounded town. General Kokott and his 26th Volksgrenadiers, reinforced by tanks and infantry of the Panzer Lehr, pressed the assault. The siege of Bastogne entered its last phase —in some ways the most perilous one for the Americans.

Kokott's plan was simple: smash into Bastogne from the southeast and the northwest, quadrants that the Germans correctly believed were lightly defended. Colonel Harper's glider troops were stretched especially thin along the entire southern perimeter of the Bastogne defenses. Only two companies, no more than 300 men in all, held a mile and a half of front between the town of Marvie and the Arlon road. On one occasion, when Harper telephoned a battalion commander to ask how well a portion of his woefully undermanned sector was defended, the officer replied sarcastically, "We have two jeeps out there."

Kokott launched his first heavy attack on Harper's men and Team O'Hara at dusk on December 23. First, German tanks blasted the already ruined town of Marvie. At about 5:30, some Panzer Lehr tanks and infantry emerged from the woods 1,000 yards off and began advancing toward a low knob south of the village, designated Hill 500 by the Americans. The hill was defended by a single U.S. infantry platoon, led by Lieutenant Stanley Morrison. Soon Germans in white camouflage snowsuits had surrounded Morrison's position in a farmhouse at the base of Hill 500. He calmly reported by phone to Colonel Harper, "Now they are all around me. I see tanks just outside my window. We are continuing to fight them back, but it looks like they have us." Morrison called back minutes later and said, "We're still holding on." Then the line went dead. That was the last ever heard from the lieutenant and his platoon.

In overrunning Hill 500, the Germans had opened a crack in Bastogne's outer defenses. The Germans sought to widen it, charging wildly toward Marvie, screaming and setting off flares that illuminated the snowy landscape. The outnumbered glider troops battled desperately against the oncom-

The bodies of German soldiers caught in a cross fire from American machine guns litter a shell-pocked open field to the northwest of Bastogne on Christmas morning, 1944. Most of the attacking infantrymen were mowed down in tight clusters as they advanced behind Mark IV tanks; others, riding on the tanks into battle, were shot off the decks. The Americans knocked out the Mark IVs soon afterward.

159

ing Germans but could not prevent them from gaining a foothold in the village. A fiery melee followed. German infantrymen closed in on a cluster of Team O'Hara's armored vehicles and flung grenades among them. One of O'Hara's 10th Armored tanks hit the fuel tank of a German self-propelled gun and turned it into a roaring torch. German guns hit a hayloft in Marvie, setting it afire. The flames outlined units of O'Hara's backup troops, who retired into the shadows. The GIs then mowed down attacking Germans, now brightly illuminated in turn by the fires.

While this battle was going on, other German units were attempting to breach Harper's line west of Marvie. German tanks rumbled to within 50 yards of the defenders' foxholes before the glider troops managed to turn them back with bazooka fire.

All of Colonel Harper's forces were now committed, and

An American jeep passes the smoldering ruins of buildings in Bastogne soon after the siege was lifted on December 26. German shelling and the fires that resulted had rendered 450 of the 1,250 houses in the town uninhabitable and had destroyed 250 more. Of the several thousand civilians trapped in the contested area, 782 had been killed.

the enemy had broken through his outer lines. But in doing so, the Germans had relaxed their pressure on other parts of the perimeter. This temporarily freed a platoon of Ewell's paratroopers and part of Team Cherry, and Lieut. Colonel Kinnard hurried both units into the area. The breach in Harper's line was plugged. Around midnight, enemy tanks tried once more to get into Marvie. One panzer, blocked by a wrecked American half-track, turned and tried to get away. But O'Hara's Shermans opened fire and wrecked the German tank. That ended General Kokott's attacks on the night of the 23rd.

Repulsed with heavy losses in the southeast, Kokott decided to deliver his knockout punch on Christmas Day from the northwest. That segment of Bastogne's circle was defended by Lieut. Colonel Chappuis and his paratroop regiment—men as yet untested in the siege of Bastogne.

December 24 was a relatively quiet day as Kokott shifted troops toward Mande-Saint Etienne, the former 101st assembly area, now lying outside the division's lines. General von Manteuffel, having been warned that units of Patton's Third Army were driving north into the German salient, sent Kokott some reinforcements—the 15th Panzer Grenadier Division. It was more urgent than ever for Manteuffel to crush American resistance in Bastogne and to capture the roads that led west.

Patton's drive was on McAuliffe's mind, too. "The finest Christmas present the 101st could get would be a relief tomorrow," he told General Middleton during a telephone call to VIII Corps headquarters in Neufchâteau. "I know, boy," Middleton replied grimly, "I know."

Christmas Eve in Bastogne started out somberly and turned into a nightmare. Two flights of Luftwaffe planes made heavy bombing raids on the town. Some bombs hit the improvised military hospital, burying 32 wounded patients in the rubble. Bastogne civilians huddled in cellars all over town. But even while the bombs were falling, an impromptu soldiers' chorus gathered in the vaulted chapel of the town's seminary, and wounded men lined the cold stone floor all the way up to the altar, wrapped in colored parachutes from the supply drops to keep warm. As the choir started singing "Silent Night, Holy Night," they joined in.

To the northwest of Bastogne, Steve Chappuis had estab-lished a comfortable command post in a stone château in the village of Rolle. He and his staff attended Christmas Mass in the château's 10th Century chapel, then enjoyed a feast made possible by Belgian civilians who contributed flour and sides of beef. At 1:30 on Christmas morning, the headquarters group went to bed, only to be awakened an hour later by heavy German artillery fire.

The German bombardment heralded Heinz Kokott's all-out attack. His plan was to hit hard at the village of Champs in Chappuis's sector and to follow with a decisive blow at the far western end of Harper's line near Flamizoulle, smashing through the thin outworks that were held by the glider troops. Kokott's tanks would then roar right into the center of Bastogne.

In the wake of the German artillery fire, white-clad Volks-grenadiers sprinted for Champs. Bursting into the village, they grappled hand-to-hand with one company of Chappuis's paratroopers. The bombardment had cut all telephone lines between Chappuis in his command post and his forward units, but the lieutenant colonel could tell from the rattle of gunfire in Champs, a mile away, that the fighting there was fierce. Still, he coolly withheld reinforcements, expecting a heavier blow to land elsewhere.

He was right. At daybreak, men of Harper's glider infantry regiment south of Champs saw 18 white-camouflaged German tanks approaching from the direction of Flamizoulle. The Mark IVs, with squads of panzer grenadiers clinging to them, roared down a snow-covered hillside, firing at the glidermen in their widely spaced foxholes.

The Americans returned the fire, then dropped deep into their foxholes as the German tanks roared right over their positions. Four GIs died and five were wounded, but the rest raised up and fought the German infantry who followed the panzers. In moments the German tanks had reached the command post of Harper's 3rd Battalion. The battalion commander, Lieut. Colonel Ray C. Allen, telephoned Harper, shouting, "They are firing point-blank at me from 150 yards range." Allen and two aides then dashed for a clump of trees, with shells from a German tank following them.

Kokott seemed to have his long-awaited breakthrough. At 5:45 Christmas morning, the leader of one of the German tank sections sent back a message saying his force was on the edge of Bastogne itself, roughly a mile from McAuliffe's command post. The other section of German tanks had split off from this group and turned northward behind the U.S. lines, hoping to take Champs and Steve Chappuis's regiment from the rear.

This was exactly what Chappuis had been waiting for. He swiftly deployed two companies of his regiment facing southward toward the oncoming Germans. He then placed some tank destroyers in a wood that lay alongside the enemy line of attack.

As the German tanks came on, the paratroopers fell back into the trees. The onrushing tanks then turned, bypassing the wood and heading for Champs, intending to roll up Chappuis's whole line of defense. As they did so, they exposed their vulnerable flanks to the tank destroyers. What followed was a slaughter. The high-velocity 76mm American guns swiftly knocked out three German tanks, and armor-piercing bazooka rockets got two more. Only one

tank made it to Champs, and it was destroyed there by a bazooka and an antitank gun.

In the meantime, the first group of tanks—heading toward Bastogne itself—ran into a maelstrom of fire from tank destroyers, artillery, bazookas, small arms and U.S. tanks. One German Mark IV was captured intact; the rest were destroyed. Of the 18 German tanks that had gone into action, not one survived. That night, Lieut. Colonel Chappuis sat down to a modest Christmas meal of sardines and crackers, secure in the knowledge that the Germans' climactic effort to take Bastogne had been smashed.

The next day brought another triumph for the defenders of Bastogne. For four days, the 4th Armored Division had been slugging its way northward to relieve the siege. On the afternoon of December 26, the lead units were only four miles south of town. They were the 37th Tank Battalion, led by Lieut. Colonel Creighton W. Abrams (who one day

would be Chief of Staff of the U.S. Army) and the 53rd Armored Infantry Battalion under Lieut. Colonel George L. Jaques. These units, along with an armored artillery battalion and a battery of 155mm howitzers, were designated Combat Command R.

The two lieutenant colonels stood on a hill overlooking the village of Clochimont, discussing their planned attack on the village of Sibret, known to be heavily defended by the Germans. Suddenly an air fleet—seemingly hundreds of cargo planes—materialized over Bastogne, dropping brightly colored parachutes and dodging puffs of enemy flak. Galvanized by this evidence of the 101st's urgent shortages—and concluding that their own battered forces were not strong enough to capture Sibret in one timely assault—Abrams and Jaques decided to take a shortcut, striking directly northward through the village of Assenois, then straight into Bastogne.

Abrams went over to his tank and radioed divisional headquarters, requesting permission to go ahead with the altered plan. In turn, 4th Armored headquarters asked Patton if he would authorize the attack, even though it risked a flank assault by Germans from Sibret. Patton answered, "I sure as hell will!"

Abrams stood up in the turret of his tank, stuck a big cigar in his mouth and announced to his men: "We're going in now. Let 'er roll!"

Dusk was settling fast. Abrams' supporting artillery sent volley after volley crashing into Assenois. The attack force started down the slope: tanks, armored cars and half-tracks filled with assault troops. Leading the way were five Cobra Kings, the new 40-ton Shermans, headed up by Lieutenant Charles Boggess.

The tanks raced into the town, their cannon and machine guns spitting fire. Troops leaped from the Cobras' decks. Shooting, bayoneting and clubbing, they worked their way from house to house. Private James R. Hendrix, a freckle-faced 19-year-old armed only with a rifle, took on the crews of two German 88mm artillery pieces that were pounding

the tanks. "Come on out!" shouted Hendrix. A German soldier poked his head up from a foxhole. Hendrix shot him in the neck. Running to the next foxhole, he found another German and smashed in his head with the butt of his M-1. Then he charged through the smoke straight at the muzzles of the two big guns. The two gun crews came out with their hands up. (Hendrix' brief one-man war would win him the Medal of Honor.)

Leaving Assenois, Lieutenant Boggess now moved toward Bastogne at top speed, with his forward machine gunner spraying the tree line along both sides of the road. When the tanks encountered a green-painted blockhouse, the lieutenant called for three quick rounds from his cannon and watched with satisfaction as the shells tore the concrete blockhouse apart.

In the gathering darkness just before 5 o'clock, Boggess saw some men duck into foxholes—but they were different: they did not look like Germans. The lieutenant took a chance. He stood up in his turret and shouted, "Come here! This is the 4th Armored!"

Slowly, suspiciously, a few helmeted heads poked out of foxholes. Then a single figure emerged and started walking toward the tanks, all the while keeping Boggess covered with his carbine. Suddenly he broke into a smile, stuck his hand up toward the turret and introduced himself: "Second Lieutenant Duane J. Webster, 326th Engineers, 101st Airborne Division."

Boggess leaned down, grinning, and shook hands. Webster asked the tankers if they had any water, explaining that his men had had nothing to drink that day but a little melted snow. The tankers produced three canteens and drank a toast in water with the paratroopers.

By this time Boggess' commanding officer, Captain William Dwight, had caught up with the lead tankers and made his way up a hill to a 101st observation post. General McAuliffe was there, waiting to greet the new arrivals. "Gee," the general said, "I am mighty glad to see you." The siege of Bastogne was lifted.

Evacuating wounded American troops from Bastogne, a column of ambulances speeds southward over a dirt road still threatened by German artillery fire. The ambulances had entered the besieged town on the heels of tanks of the 4th Armored Division on the 27th of December.

TANKERS TO THE RESCUE

Late in their drive to relieve Bastogne, tank crews of the U.S. 4th Armored Division watch planes preparing to air-drop supplies to the defenders of the town.

FIVE DAYS TO CLOSE A 22-MILE GAP

Square-jawed General McAuliffe (right) held out in Bastogne for eight days before Lieut. Colonel Abrams' unit broke through to lift the siege.

The 101st Airborne Division had been defending Bastogne for three days when, on December 22, 1944, its commanding officer, Brigadier General Anthony C. McAuliffe, received some heartening news by radio. The message said, "Hugh is coming," and it meant that Major General Hugh J. Gaffey and his 4th Armored Division were on their way to relieve the siege.

Gaffey's message, sent from the vicinity of Arlon, about 20 miles south of Bastogne, joined the two divisions in spirit even as they fought their separate battles. The paratroopers of the 101st Airborne, ordered by their corps commander, General Middleton, to "hold at all costs," kept glancing to the south and rooting the 4th onward while they held off the attacks of three German divisions. The tankers of the 4th Armored, with orders from Third Army commander George Patton to "drive like hell," were driven even harder by the knowledge of the 101st's plight.

If the 4th Armored had met with only routine resistance, it might have fought through to Bastogne in a day or two. But the division's three combat commands were opposed by the crack German 5th Parachute Division, along with elements of several other units and a generous complement of high-velocity antitank guns. The tankers also had to contend with swirling snow and fog, German mines, road-blocking shell craters, deep mud and—after a quick freeze on December 23—mirror-like ice, whose blinding glare hindered drivers and gunners. The division fought for five days, grinding out the slow advances that are mapped on the following pages, before Lieut. Colonel Creighton W. Abrams' battalion of Combat Command R finally burst into the Bastogne perimeter.

The dramatic linkup was completed at a high cost—about 1,000 men dead in the 4th Armored, almost 2,000 dead in Bastogne. But paratroopers of the 101st Airborne, who had proudly dubbed themselves "the Battered Bastards of the Bastion of Bastogne," were annoyed that everyone in the Allied camp had been worried about them. McAuliffe said, "We're in fine shape: We're ready to take the offensive."

Half-tracks of the 4th Armored make their way to the outskirts of Bastogne while the division's artillery blasts the German positions into smoking ruins.

DECEMBER 22

On the first day of the 4th Armored's attack to relieve the 101st Airborne, Combat Command A reached Martelange and Combat Command B advanced to Burnon. But Germans continued to hold out in both villages.

In Bastogne's old walled cemetery, German prisoners dig graves for dead GIs, some of whom are frozen in grotesque postures. The American defenders captured 649 enemy soldiers in the course of the siege.

When the 4th Armored Division started its drive northward to rescue the 101st, the tankers were highly optimistic; the distance, after all, was not great. "The general impression," said a tank colonel, "was that we could just cut our way through." Once they had cut through, they planned to hold open a supply corridor to Bastogne until the siege was relieved.

The fact was that the hopes of both divisions for a quick linkup were doomed even before the tankers ran into the first German outpost. The two spearhead units of the 4th Armored, Combat Commands A and B, made good progress through deepening snow on the 22nd. Combat Command A advanced eight miles to Martelange. Combat Command B drove 12 miles north to Burnon and then won a hot midnight fight. "Tanks moved up the road," one officer recalled, "and literally blasted their way through the enemy fire from 75s, bazookas and machine guns."

However, German resistance was stiffening, and at the end of the day both combat commands found themselves stopped by bridges that had been blown.

In Bastogne, meanwhile, the paratroopers buried their dead and then dug themselves in and waited.

Combat Commands A and B gained only two miles each in hard fighting; Combat Command R advanced five miles to Bigonville.

Wounded GIs crowd the floor of a makeshift hospital in Bastogne. The aid station was moved several times after having been shelled.

A pathfinder, parachuted into Bastogne, mans a radar atop a pile of bricks and directs supply planes to the surrounded town.

Map labels:

Belgium

Luxembourg

Bastogne

Sibret

Assenois

Clochimont

Hompré

Wiltz

Remichampagne

Chaumont

Remonville

Bercheux

Hollange

Burnon

Tintange

Warnach

Sûre River

Neufchâteau

Bigonville

Martelange

Ettelbruck

COMBAT COMMAND R

COMBAT COMMAND B

COMBAT COMMAND A

Quatre Vents

Habay-la-Neuve

Arlon

- - - U.S. FORCES DEFENSE PERIMETER

← U.S. 4TH ARMORED DIV. ATTACK

0   Scale of Miles   5

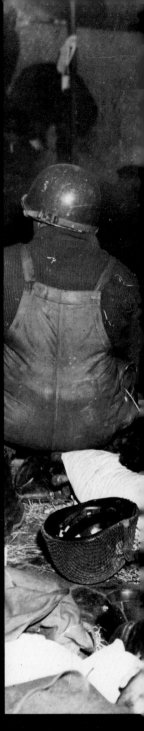

The weather broke on the 23rd, bringing Bastogne 241 U.S. cargo planes with desperately needed supplies, especially artillery rounds and medicines for the wounded, who had suffered for four days without painkillers or antiseptics. But for the 4th Armored, that day was a bitter one of small gains achieved at high cost.

A leading unit of Combat Command A fought for hours in German-held Martelange while engineers erected a 90-foot Bailey bridge across the deep gorge of the Sûre River. Then the command pushed forward to the well-defended village of Warnach, where German troops repulsed several assaults and inflicted heavy casualties.

Combat Command B followed an almost identical scenario. Having built a bridge at Burnon, the GIs pushed forward to Chaumont, then captured the village. But German self-propelled guns roared out of a nearby wood, blasting 11 Shermans into flaming junk. "We were ordered to withdraw," reported an infantry sergeant. "We

found a wounded tanker and Pvt. William McIlvaine had ahold of him and was pulling, helping him back. We went by another of our tankers sitting in a ditch. His foot was shot off. He saw we couldn't take him too. He just said, 'Hi'ya fellas.' We were the last out."

The only encouraging move of the day was made by the division's reserve, Combat Command R. This unit, advancing parallel to Combat Command A, drove to Bigonville to protect the right flank.

DECEMBER 24

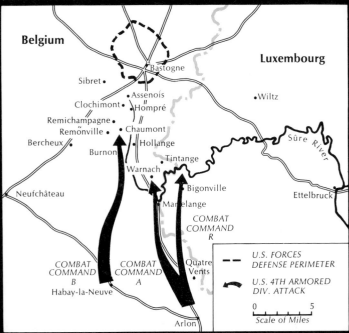

Belgium

Luxembourg

Bastogne
Sibret
Assenois
Clochimont • Hompré
Remichampagne •
Remonville • Chaumont
Bercheux • Hollange
Burnon • Tintange
Warnach
Neufchâteau • Bigonville
Marvelange
Sûre River
Ettelbruck
Wiltz

COMBAT
COMMAND
R

COMBAT
COMMAND
B
COMBAT
COMMAND
A
Quatre
Vents

Habay-la-Neuve

Arlon

– – – U.S. FORCES
DEFENSE PERIMETER

U.S. 4TH ARMORED
DIV. ATTACK

0   5
Scale of Miles

Combat Command A's drive was held up by stiff German resistance in Warnach while B continued its inconclusive fight for Chaumont. After a long fight, Combat Command R captured Bigonville at 11 a.m.

On December 24 the Bastogne perimeter was ominously quiet. GI defenders spotted German units shifting westward and braced themselves for new assaults from that direction. McAuliffe, still hoping for relief as a holiday present for his men, radioed the 4th Armored, "There is only one more shopping day before Christmas."

But neither McAuliffe's reminder nor angry orders from General Patton himself—"Bypass these towns!"—could move the 4th Armored to any greater effort. Combat Command A had to battle all day to drive a relatively short distance past Warnach. Combat Command B struggled all day to recapture Chaumont, but was repulsed by powerful German tank and infantry forces. The division's reserve, Combat Command R, drove into Bigonville, where an enemy infantry battalion was holed up. "The Germans fought stubbornly," reported a tank officer, "and surrendered only when they had no more ammunition."

Crowded into a makeshift chapel, men of the 101st Airborne sing Christmas carols at midnight. The service came to an abrupt end when Luftwaffe bombs exploded in the street outside.

A gunner of Combat Command R makes his breakfast in a foxhole near his 155mm howitzer after an all-night battle at Bigonville.

Combat engineers use mine detectors to clear a road of German mines, enabling 4th Armored vehicles to advance closer to Bastogne.

DECEMBER 25

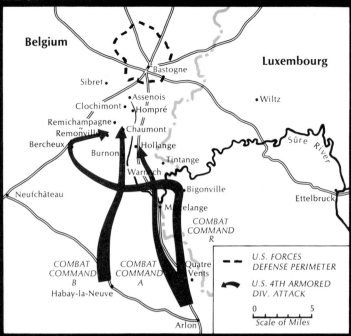

On Christmas Day, Combat Command A drove past Tintange toward Hollange, B recaptured Chaumont, and R swung west to Remonville.

At dawn on Christmas Day, 18 German tanks and two infantry battalions crashed through the Americans' perimeter northwest of Bastogne. But the men of the 101st quickly rebuilt their defense line. Supported by tank destroyers and artillery, they drove back the last and heaviest German attack on the town.

Just a few miles to the southwest, the 4th Armored Division's three combat commands were spoiling to join the fight in Bastogne. But German machine gunners and antitank-gun crews concealed in the woods raked the tanks and men of the 4th as they crossed fields. Other German units defended roadblocks to the death. By early evening, however, Combat Command R had blasted the enemy out of Remonville, and its hard-bitten commander, Creighton Abrams, prepared to take up his favorite position—"way out on the goddamn point of the attack"—while his last 20 Shermans blasted their way into Bastogne.

Glancing at the forms of two dead comrades, paratroopers of the 101st Airborne walk past a water tower among the bomb-damaged buildings of Bastogne. The dead paratroopers had been killed during the heavy Luftwaffe raid the night before.

Crawling forward under German machine-gun fire, soldiers of the 4th Armored Division cross a field about five miles from Bastogne.

One of Combat Command R's light tanks churns past the corpse of a German soldier who was killed by the tank's machine gunner.

Map legend:
- - - U.S. FORCES DEFENSE PERIMETER
→ U.S. 4TH ARMORED DIV. ATTACK

0   5
Scale of Miles

Map labels: Belgium, Luxembourg, Sibret, Bastogne, Clochimont, Assenois, Hompré, Remichampagne, Remonville, Chaumont, Wiltz, Berchaux, Hollange, Burnon, Sûre River, Tintange, Warnach, Bigonville, Neufchâteau, Ettelbruck, Martelange, Quatre Vents, COMBAT COMMAND R, COMBAT COMMAND B, COMBAT COMMAND A, Habay-la-Neuve, Arlon

While Combat Commands A and B continued to make slow progress, Combat Command R took Remichampagne and later Clochimont. Finally Abrams and his lead tanks plowed through Assenois into Bastogne.

Paratroopers of the 101st Airborne Division share a bottle of wine with a private of the 4th Armored Division (right front) in an impromptu celebration following the linkup that finally broke the siege of Bastogne.

A rifleman, a machine gunner and tanks of the 4th Armored fight to hold open the corridor to Bastogne against counterattacking Germans. A tanker said that the corridor was "so narrow you can spit across it."

6

"Old Gravel Voice" unleashes "Hell on Wheels"
The Shermans stage a bloody ambush
A festive dinner of roast swan
2nd Armored vs. 2nd Panzer
A farsighted major buys time at a way-stop
Montgomery straightens the line
Hitler adds a "Great Blow" to the big attack
Squeezing the Bulge
Eisenhower's showdown with Montgomery
How Churchill set the record straight

On December 23, 1944, Major General Ernest N. Harmon, commander of the U.S. 2nd Armored Division, sat down to a pleasant lunch with his staff at their new command post in a snug Ardennes château in the village of Havelange, 19 miles east of the Meuse River. Harmon and his "Hell On Wheels" division, part of the U.S. VII Corps, had arrived in the Ardennes just the day before, following a forced march of 70 miles from the Aachen area. His weary men needed a few days rest, and they seemed certain to get it.

To the east, fighting swirled through the Ardennes, and the Allied prospects remained uncertain: Although the two shoulders of the American defense remained firm, Saint-Vith had fallen, the town of Bastogne hung by a thread, and German units in the center of the front had broken loose and were galloping for the Meuse. But Field Marshal Montgomery, now in command of American troops in the northern half of the Ardennes, had passed down word that the VII Corps was to assemble in the open country around Havelange, avoid contact with the enemy and prepare for a counterattack when the German drive had spent itself. Harmon was told by his corps commander, Major General J. Lawton Collins, not to expect any action for at least a week, perhaps 10 days.

Over lunch, Harmon conveyed this happy news to his officers, who relaxed at the prospect of a respite from fighting. They ate, and were sipping coffee when a young and very excited officer pushed his way into the room. Lieutenant Everett C. Jones was wearing a bloody bandage around his head, and he bore the startling information that Germans were close at hand. A reconnaissance patrol led by Jones had been fired on by tanks just an hour earlier 10 miles to the south. His armored car had been hit, but he and the crew had managed to escape.

Jones's news electrified Harmon. If the Germans were 10 miles due south, they were within artillery range of the Meuse. Harmon reacted in a manner befitting his reputation as one of the Army's most aggressive combat leaders. He jumped up from the table, ran across a snowy field to a grove of trees where a tank battalion was bivouacked and asked the tank commander how long it would take him to get his outfit on the road. Five minutes, the commander replied, provided radio silence was lifted.

"Radio silence is lifted here and now," said Harmon in

THE GERMAN HIGH TIDE

the throaty growl that had earned him the nickname "Old Gravel Voice." "You get down that road and start fighting. The whole damned division is coming right behind you."

In five minutes, the lead company of Shermans was rolling south. A little later, another contingent of tanks rumbled southeastward. Seventeen miles below them, stretched out in a column 12 miles long, lay the 2nd Panzer Division—the vanguard of the German offensive.

No other German division had gained as much ground in the Ardennes as the 2nd Panzer. Its success was the fruit of a simple expedient—avoiding prolonged entanglements. The 2nd Panzer had begun its current trek by shooting the gap between Saint-Vith and Bastogne, brushing the Bastogne perimeter at Noville, which it cleared of Americans in a day of fierce fighting. When it became apparent that Bastogne would not fall easily, the 2nd Panzer resumed its westward journey *(map, page 181)*. On December 23 the division skirted the U.S.-held town of Marche, and by that evening its leading elements were within 15 miles of the Meuse.

But the very success of the 2nd Panzer in closing on the Meuse had exposed it to danger. It was traveling alone, having outdistanced the friendly forces on either flank: the 116th Panzer Division on the north and the Panzer Lehr Division to the south. Both of those units had had less luck in negotiating the blown bridges and roadblocks in their path westward, so the more ground the 2nd Panzer gained, the more vulnerable it became to American jabs along its flanks. By December 23, moreover, it was badly strung out; its men were numb with exhaustion and they were running out of fuel for their tanks.

No one realized more clearly that General von Manteuffel the precarious situation of the 2nd Panzer. But he was obsessed with the idea of reaching the Meuse. Attaining that elusive goal would go far to make up for the frustrations and delays of the Ardennes offensive. Manteuffel ordered the Panzer Lehr to break off its attack in the Bastogne area and make its way forward to join the 2nd Panzer for the final push to the Meuse. On December 23 he personally led the Panzer Lehr from Saint-Hubert to the Rochefort area, about 15 miles from the river. But the 116th Panzer Division was still in trouble. That evening, restless and angry, Manteuffel visited the 116th to spur it forward to protect the exposed northern flank of the 2nd Panzer.

All of Manteuffel's efforts to strengthen the German salient came too late. Before daylight on December 24, the punch that General Harmon had aimed at the head of the 2nd Panzer struck home. One of the task forces that he had sent southward collided with an outriding 2nd Panzer column probing to the north.

The results were spectacular. A jeep patrol riding ahead of the American tanks heard the rumble of approaching armor and raced back to warn the column. Lieut. Colonel Hugh R. O'Farrell, the task-force commander, had barely enough time to order his Shermans off the road and into a concealing grove of trees. When the German column appeared, the Americans opened up with machine guns and tank cannon, catching the panzers completely by surprise. The German tanks that were hit bled flaming fuel, lighting up the darkness and immeasurably aiding the marksmanship of the 2nd Armored ambushers. In the garish light, the American gunners pounded the Germans until the entire column was annihilated. The engagement was a stunning success for the 2nd Armored, but it was merely the opening round in a great tank battle.

Later that morning, the vanguard of the 2nd Panzer Division was rolling through the fog toward Celles, a village just four miles from the Meuse. The tanks, now critically low on gas, stopped at about 6 a.m. to verify road conditions and directions at the Pavillon Ardennais, a pleasant inn run by Madame Marthe Monrique. All she had seen were a few American engineers laying a single chain of mines across the road before retreating headlong in their jeeps, but Mme. Monrique told the Germans convincingly that the Americans had been working day and night mining the road for miles ahead, and that there were thousands of enemy soldiers waiting for them just over the hill. Alarmed by her tale, the German officers ordered the column to pull off the road into a forest and to hole up there for the night. Once more a bold bit of misinformation had caused the German forces an expensive delay.

That afternoon, Harmon called VII Corps headquarters again. "One of my patrols just spotted Kraut tanks coiled up near Celles," Gravel Voice rasped excitedly. "Belgians say the Krauts are out of gas. They're sitting ducks. Let me take the bastards!" The American command was still worried about Montgomery's orders to avoid contact with German forces until the American lines could be put in order. After much deliberation at VII Corps headquarters, Harmon was authorized to make the attack. Gravel Voice hollered into the telephone, "The bastards are in the bag!"

At 8 o'clock on Christmas morning, the 2nd Armored Division launched an all-out attack against the panzers at the western tip of the Bulge. Combat Command B, under Brigadier General I. D. White, plunged southwest toward Celles, bent on encircling and destroying the enemy tank concentration there. At the same time, Combat Command A, under Brigadier General John H. Collier, drove down to the southeast toward the town of Rochefort to stop any further German advances toward the Meuse. Harmon spent Christmas Day visiting forward units and urging them on.

It was 10 o'clock in the evening when Harmon finally sat down to dinner at the château. Fortunately, he had taken steps to see that Christmas dinner would be appropriately festive. The morning before, he had spotted a swan serenely gliding around a pond at the château. On Christmas Eve, Harmon had instructed his jeep driver to shoot the swan with his carbine and deliver it to the mess sergeant. When the swan was brought out on a platter for Harmon and the staff officers at the command post, some of the diners eyed the big bird suspiciously, but Harmon pitched in with gusto and the others followed suit. The swan was acclaimed as deliciously ducklike, and when Harmon went to the kitchen for a snack at midnight, he found the carcass stripped clean.

The fight to annihilate the 2nd Panzer troops in the Celles pocket was a mosaic of small actions, and it raged for three days. At one point, American tanks south of Celles were attacked by 45-ton Panther and 57-ton Tiger tanks of the Panzer Lehr Division, which was trying to break through to rescue the trapped troops. The men of the 2nd Armored had learned from hard experience that their Sherman tanks could not stop these monsters—but that fighter-bombers could. As it happened, some rocket-firing British Typhoons were stationed close by, and while American artillery held off the enemy tanks, General White paid a quick visit to the British near Dinant to enlist their aid.

The British pilots were eager to join the Americans in the battle, but they expressed concern because the 2nd Ar-

mored had no way to communicate with the planes and guide them to the targets. White proposed to send up Piper Cubs with artillery observers who knew where the tanks were located and could lead the Typhoons to them. To this the British agreed.

Shortly afterward, the men of the 2nd Armored were treated to a gratifying aerial show. A squadron of Typhoons flew over, honing in on a single Piper Cub. The Cub dived low enough to point out the tanks. Then the Typhoons swooped down with rockets blazing, leaving a trail of burning hulks in their wake.

The Panzer Lehr made two other attempts to rescue the 2nd Panzer Division from the pocket. Both efforts were stopped by Typhoons and by P-38 fighter-bombers called in by radio. The 116th Panzer Division also tried to fight its way to the west and join in the attack toward the Meuse, but the division ran into units of the U.S. 84th Infantry Division at Verdenne. The 116th was worn down in a hard struggle and forced to dig in. It was finished as an offensive threat in the Battle of the Bulge.

Elements of yet another German division—the 9th Panzer—were thrust into the whorl of combat at the tip of the Bulge. The 9th Panzer units seized control of the road junction at Humain, a village northeast of Rochefort, and they hung on tenaciously in hopes that they could continue their westward thrust to the Meuse River. For 24 hours the Germans took a terrible pounding from artillery and tanks of the surrounding 2nd Armored Division, but they refused to give in or retreat. Finally, on December 27, General Harmon threw his reserve combat command into the attack on Humain, and after a day of raging battle, the village fell to the Americans.

"The Germans' last gasp came just after sundown," Harmon wrote later. "A few survivors had found refuge in a thick-walled castle on the edge of town. They resisted all efforts to get them out and refused to surrender. Then a flamethrowing tank belonging to the British was brought forward. It belched its geyser of flame into a large tree just in front of the castle. In a moment the tree was a high torch that lighted the courtyard like day, and very shortly it had shriveled to ash.

"This spectacular exhibition proved to be effective propaganda. A few minutes later, 200 German soldiers marched out of the castle with their hands held high. They had seen enough."

Later that night, Harmon sat down in the wreckage of a farmhouse near Celles and wrote a brief report of the battle to VII Corps headquarters: "Attached is a list of spoils we took—including some 1,200 prisoners. Killed and wounded some 2,500. A great slaughter." Harmon listed a fearful tally of machines and weaponry destroyed or captured by the 2nd Armored and the American and British warplanes. The total included 82 tanks, 83 field guns and 441 vehicles.

More important, one arm of the German offensive had been smashed, and the attacking forces had yet to seize a bridgehead on the Meuse.

While the tank battle at the tip of the Bulge was unfolding, the Germans were mounting another threat some 40 miles to the east, at a tiny, isolated crossroads called Baraque de Fraiture. From this hamlet, a broad, paved highway—a perfect tank route—led to the north. Opening the highway would present the Germans with two extremely enticing alternatives: they could follow it through the towns of Manhay and Werbomont and on to the city of Liège; or, at Manhay, they could wheel westward on another road and attack in support of Manteuffel's breakthrough. The unit appointed to gain access to the highway was the 2nd SS Panzer Division, which had been brought from the vicinity of Elsenborn Ridge after General Dietrich's attacks had been stymied there. For a while, the 2nd SS Panzer had served on the right flank of Manteuffel's Fifth Panzer Army, but as Manteuffel's tanks rolled westward, the division had peeled off and thrust northwest, aiming straight for the crossroads at Baraque de Fraiture.

The road junction was situated atop a 2,139-foot plateau

and lay along the boundary between the American 82nd Airborne and 3rd Armored Divisions. Both divisions were stretched thin, and no one had assumed responsibility for the crossroads until an enterprising major named Arthur C. Parker III happened along. And thereby hung an unlikely set of circumstances.

Major Parker and a handful of his men were the surviving members of an artillery battalion of the 106th Division. When the German offensive struck, Parker's outfit was far out on the Schnee Eifel ridge, protruding into German territory. All the rest of the men in his battalion, the 589th, had been killed or captured. But Parker had led his men off the ridge and struggled westward, buffeted by the shifting tides of battle, until he reached Baraque de Fraiture.

At the crossroads, Parker saw only a few crude stone houses surrounded by pine forests, but a glance at his map showed him clearly—as clearly as it had shown the German High Command—that Baraque de Fraiture was a crucial junction. So Parker stopped retreating then and there. He immediately set up three howitzers to cover the road junction, and he began collaring a ragtag assortment of retreating troops to help out—units that included four half-tracks armed with .50-caliber machine guns, 11 Sherman tanks and a reconnaissance platoon of the 3rd Armored Division.

Parker's scratch outfit withstood a number of probes by enemy patrols. Word of these hit-and-run attacks reached Major General James M. Gavin, commander of the 82nd Airborne, who recognized that if the Germans broke through at Baraque de Fraiture and thrust northward, the 82nd Airborne would be in grave danger, its flank turned and enemy soldiers in its rear area.

Gavin dispatched a company of glider troops to reinforce Parker's motley group at Baraque de Fraiture; he also sent a

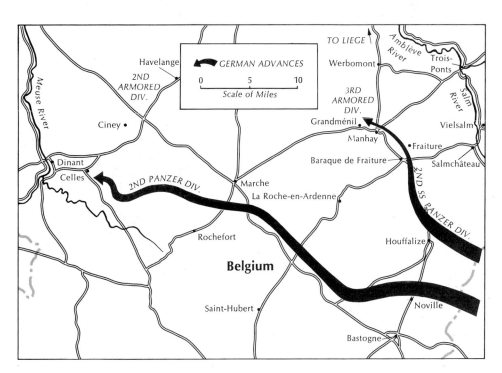

Striking westward, the 2nd Panzer Division skirted Bastogne, bypassed the American-held town of Marche and rolled on to Celles, four miles from its first objective, the Meuse River. Near Celles, the spearhead was encircled and trapped by the U.S. 2nd Armored Division. In the meantime, the 2nd SS Panzer Division drove northwest to Manhay, where it wheeled westward. At Grandménil, it was halted by the American 3rd Armored Division.

glider battalion to the town of Fraiture, about a mile northeast of the crossroads. These two units arrived on the morning of December 22, just in time to meet the first contingent of the 2nd SS Panzer. The panzer troops began their appointed task before dawn on the 23rd by testing the defense at Fraiture with a small assault force, which the glidermen were able to throw back. In the afternoon the Germans turned serious. For 20 minutes their artillery pounded the American positions around the crossroads; then, preceded by two companies of tanks, a panzer-grenadier regiment attacked. The Americans, heavily outnumbered, stood their ground for more than an hour. In the end their positions were overwhelmed. Only 44 of Gavin's original 116 glidermen at the crossroads managed to escape; the rest were killed or captured.

Major Parker was seriously wounded in the fighting, but his valiant stand at Baraque de Fraiture delayed the Germans and provided time the Americans desperately needed to bring in troops to stop the enemy drive. GIs in the

Bulge renamed Baraque de Fraiture "Parker's Crossroads."

As the junction was falling to the Germans, General Gavin received some news that confirmed his worst suspicions about the enemy's intentions in that sector. Orders found on a captured German regimental adjutant indicated that the 2nd SS Panzer Division was embarking on a major thrust north toward Manhay. The threat to the weak right flank of the 82nd Airborne was as severe as Gavin had feared.

His troubles mounting by the hour, Gavin rushed a reserve battalion to the highway north of Baraque de Fraiture to stop the German tanks from rolling up his airborne division's right flank. The general became even more alarmed when he drove to Manhay to confer with officers at the 3rd Armored command post there—and discovered that the town was completely abandoned except for one lonely MP on duty at the crossroads. Gavin hurried to the headquarters of the XVIII Airborne Corps and asked for reinforcements. Then, even though he knew it would stretch his front line to the breaking point, he ordered Colonel Reuben

H. Tucker of the 504th Parachute Infantry Regiment to move his headquarters and one of his battalions west to intercept the German drive.

During the night, XVIII Airborne Corps headquarters realized how dangerous the situation was, and turned over Combat Command B of the 9th Armored Division to Gavin. Elements of the 3rd Armored and the 7th Armored, the weary troops retreating from Saint-Vith, were also ordered to reinforce the airborne troops. And Tucker was instructed to move the rest of his regiment—except for a small detachment—to the right flank as fast as possible.

As the reinforcements poured into the path of the Germans on the morning of December 24 and fighting raged along the contested highway, Field Marshal Montgomery drove up to the farmhouse headquarters of the XVIII Airborne Corps. His appearance on the scene presaged a major alteration in the American defensive plan. The imperturbable Montgomery had come to "tidy" the front line, as he put it, by giving up some ground.

At this point, the 82nd Airborne Division was stretched over a front of more than 15 miles. Moreover, its line was crazily angled, running from north to south along the west bank of the Salm River, then extending due west. The clumsy, dog-legged line had been selected originally to cover the withdrawal of the 7th Armored Division from Saint-Vith. However, the withdrawal had been completed the night before, and Montgomery thought it more important for the 82nd to withdraw to a strong, consolidated position than to cling to real estate as a matter of honor. Gavin protested Montgomery's plan, arguing that airborne troops were used to fighting in surrounded positions where they were under orders not to yield an inch. The 82nd Airborne Division had never retreated in its history, and Gavin was concerned that a retreat might have a disastrous effect on the division's morale.

His argument failed to sway his superiors, however; that night, as units of the 3rd and 7th Armored Divisions took over the defense of Manhay, commanders of the airborne division reconnoitered new defensive positions on high ground to the north. Then they carried out the withdrawal in the darkness. Although some of the tough airborne troops grumbled about the retreat, there was no loss of

morale, as Gavin had feared. In fact the operation, a risky venture in the darkness, went off smartly. Bridges across the Salm River were blown; minefields were planted and roadblocks set up to cover the withdrawal. The 508th Regiment, deployed near Vielsalm, was attacked in force and had to fall back under heavy pressure—an intricate maneuver it executed with few losses. The covering force at the village of Thier-du-Mont was cut off, but managed to break out and fight its way back to the main body of the division without the loss of a single man.

By Christmas morning, all regiments of the 82nd were dug in at their new positions; mines were being planted and wire strung. Then, on December 27, two German divisions attacked in great force east of Manhay, infantrymen yelling and firing their weapons as they charged the positions of the 82nd. The Germans expected that the defenders would break and run. But the paratroopers stood their ground even though one battalion was overrun. A reserve company was quickly called to the front and was able to tip the balance, finally forcing the Germans back. The German assault had been ferocious, however, and if Montgomery had not insisted on straightening and tightening the 82nd's line, the outcome might have been disastrous.

Nevertheless, the withdrawal of the 82nd severely weakened the American position at Manhay. Units of the 3rd and 7th Armored Divisions that remained to defend the town became confused and uncoordinated under German pressure; even as the paratroopers were withdrawing, the defense of Manhay crumbled and the Germans took the town. With good reason, the American commanders continued to worry that the Germans would break out to the north and go on to Liège. But to their amazement and relief, the German force at Manhay, instead of continuing to attack north, pivoted and launched a drive to the west, intent on relieving some of the pressure on the 2nd Panzer Division trapped in the pocket at Celles.

In their new westward push, the Germans took the town of Grandménil, a mile from Manhay, but they were later driven out by counterattacking forces of the 3rd Armored Division. Meanwhile, General Ridgway, the XVIII Airborne Corps commander, ordered the badly depleted 7th Armored Division to attack from the north and retake Manhay. The 7th Armored, bloodied and exhausted, was slow

Soldiers of the 2nd SS Panzer Division trudge past burning American vehicles near a vital road junction at Manhay. Late on Christmas Eve, the German troops drove the American defenders out of the village, enabling the Germans to open a route westward toward the Meuse River.

getting started and was delayed by felled trees along the road. Concerned by the delay, Ridgway decided to throw in a fresh battalion of the 517th Parachute Infantry Regiment, and in the early morning hours of December 27, the paratroopers captured Manhay. The Germans had reached the high-water marks of the Battle of the Bulge at Celles in the west and Manhay in the north. Hitler's great gamble had failed. Not a single German tank crossed the Meuse.

But the Battle of the Bulge was far from over. Though the great German counteroffensive had reached its maximum penetration during the first 10 days, the Allied forces faced an enormous task in containing it completely and then pushing the German armies back. Battered and weary, the Allies would have to fight not only against skilled and stubborn soldiers, many of them experienced in winter warfare from long months on the Russian front, but against the grim enemy of winter itself.

Top commanders on both sides, aware that the struggle was taking a decisive turn, had been reshaping their strategies to fit the new outline of the Ardennes battlefield. In the American camp, an aggressive mood prevailed. General Bradley believed that the Germans had shot their bolt and that the time was ripe for an all-out counteroffensive. But the ever-cautious Montgomery was not so sanguine. He pointed out that the U.S. First Army—still under his control on the northern half of the Bulge—had suffered heavy losses and would have to be reinforced before it could go over to the offensive.

The American field commanders chafed at Montgomery's inaction, but the field marshal was determined to wait until the First Army was in better shape. In the meantime, the U.S. Third Army busied itself with efforts to widen the lifeline to Bastogne and to maneuver into a better position to strike northward.

While the Americans were preparing to switch over to the offensive, German commanders were also revising their strategy. The failure of their efforts to cross the Meuse had forced them to lower their sights. They proposed that instead of driving for Antwerp, the Fifth and Sixth Panzer

Armies concentrate on destroying the American units located east of the river.

Hitler, unchastened by the obvious shortcomings of his offensive, clung to his dream of capturing the big prize, Antwerp. He grudgingly agreed to confine the offensive to the east of the Meuse—but as a temporary measure only. Once his armies trapped and crippled the American forces there, they would again set their sights on Antwerp. Hitler reminded his generals that Bastogne was still a painful thorn in the German side. German success, east or west of the Meuse, hinged on the capture of that crucial crossroads. "Above all," he said in a warning to his commanders, "we must have Bastogne!"

The Führer, in the meantime, had authorized two grandiose schemes aimed at relieving pressure on the Ardennes offensive. The first of these, called "The Great Blow," was a plan to launch hundreds of fighters—most of the remaining Luftwaffe—against enemy air bases in the west, eliminating the air power that was proving so lethal in the Ardennes.

The Führer unleashed his massive strike at 8 o'clock on New Year's morning, sending his warplanes into the air over Belgium, Holland and northern France. They streaked in just above the treetops and savagely pounded the Allied airfields for two hours. In one sense, The Great Blow was a huge success: by 10 a.m. a number of bases and 206 Allied aircraft had been destroyed or damaged. But it was virtual suicide; the Luftwaffe suffered the crippling loss of 300 planes and 253 trained fighter pilots. "The German losses were so high," wrote Hitler's official diary keeper, Major Schramm, "that continuation of such attacks had to be given up." In fact, damage to the Luftwaffe was such that it would never again take to the skies in appreciable numbers.

New Year's Day also saw another German operation: *Nordwind* (North Wind), a diversionary scheme to lure American Third Army troops away from Bastogne by striking elsewhere, far to the southeast of Belgium in the Vosges Mountains and the plains of Alsace. There, the U.S. Sixth Army Group, under Lieut. General Jacob L. Devers, had driven a salient all the way to the Rhine; in the process, French troops under his command had captured the great

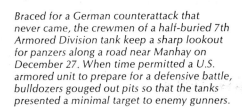

Braced for a German counterattack that never came, the crewmen of a half-buried 7th Armored Division tank keep a sharp lookout for panzers along a road near Manhay on December 27. When time permitted a U.S. armored unit to prepare for a defensive battle, bulldozers gouged out pits so that the tanks presented a minimal target to enemy gunners.

A bespectacled Hitler reviews "The Great Blow"—his plan for a mammoth air strike in support of the Ardennes offensive—with Reich Marshal Hermann Göring (front left), General Heinz Guderian (front right) and other high-ranking officers on January 1, 1945. The actual strike was effective but costly. Said Luftwaffe Major General Adolf Galland, "We sacrificed our last substance."

Alsatian city of Strasbourg. South of Strasbourg, however, German troops still held a bridgehead west of the river, around the city of Colmar. Hitler's plan of attack called for German spearheads to cut off Strasbourg and link up with forces in the Colmar pocket, as it was called.

The intelligence officers of the U.S. Seventh Army anticipated the attack and warned Generals Devers and Eisenhower. Ike suggested that Devers withdraw from the threatened area rather than risk the entrapment of his troops. This plan had one major drawback—it meant that the French would lose Strasbourg again. Nevertheless, when the Germans attacked toward the city on New Year's Eve, Eisenhower ordered the pullback. When the French were informed of this scheme, they erupted in a Gallic furor. Strasbourg had been under German control from 1870 to 1918, and again from 1940 until its liberation in November 1944. The French were fearful of reprisals against the city's 400,000 inhabitants if the Germans returned. Indeed, so alarming was this prospect that the French threatened to remove their forces from Allied control and defend Strasbourg on their own.

The delicate problem was quickly bucked all the way up to Roosevelt and Churchill. Roosevelt refused to become involved, but Churchill discussed the issue in Versailles with Eisenhower, General de Gaulle and General Alphonse-Pierre Juin, chief of staff of the French Ministry of Defense.

The Allied leaders decided at the conference to bow to French wishes and retract the order to abandon Strasbourg. The Allied lines would be shortened, but the city would remain within the area to be defended.

As it turned out, stubborn Allied resistance prevented the Germans from linking up their forces. Strasbourg was saved, and Operation *Nordwind*, which failed to achieve Hitler's aim of diverting American troops from the Ardennes, petered out in less than three weeks.

In the meantime, the Allies were girding for a final great offensive of their own in the Ardennes, a pincer movement designed to cut off the Bulge at its waist. The U.S. First Army would attack from the north, the U.S. Third Army would push up from Bastogne in the south, and the two armies would meet at the village of Houffalize, trapping all the German forces in the tip of the Bulge.

Patton's VIII Corps, west of Bastogne, launched its attack on December 30, with the spearhead, the 11th Armored

Division, driving north toward Houffalize. On the next day, east of Bastogne, his III Corps, led by the 6th Armored Division, struck northeast toward Saint-Vith.

The American attack west of Bastogne made good progress on the morning of December 30, but as the tanks pushed north, they collided with German panzers attacking toward Bastogne. Withering artillery fire forced the Americans to sideslip farther west, and at Moircy, American infantrymen of the 87th Division ran into heavy fire from tanks, machine guns, small arms and artillery. All the momentum of the attack drained away.

On the east side of Bastogne, the 6th Armored ground painfully forward through Wardin, Neffe and Bizory—a roll call of battles that had been fought earlier by the 101st Airborne Division. Roadways were covered with ice, tanks slipped and slid, and fighter-bombers were grounded by snow flurries. The 6th Armored Division suffered heavy casualties, and farther east troops of the 26th Division, attacking toward Wiltz, had to contend not only with bitter enemy resistance but also with extremely difficult terrain—rugged hills, ravines and icy streams.

All around Bastogne the Germans fought with ferocity, blocking the Third Army's move north with short, sharp counterattacks of their own. German strength was formidable; by New Year's Day, eight divisions were in the area, and they were still determined to take Bastogne. So even as Patton's troops surged northward, the Germans continued to throw massive forces against the Americans around that embattled citadel. Although the Germans did not get the

town, they raised havoc with the Third Army's assault, slowing the march of Patton's troops almost to a halt.

On January 3, the upper claw of the Allied pincer began to move, with First Army units striking on a 35-mile front from the north and elements of the British XXX Corps attacking from the west. The troops found the going rough. Abominable weather with freezing temperatures limited their advances to two miles a day at best; day after day, soldiers wallowed haplessly through the snowdrifts, and tanks and half-tracks skewed crazily on the icy roads. The GIs learned to save their hands and feet from frostbite by cutting crude patterns from blankets and sewing them together for makeshift mittens and foot warmers; they stuffed sheets of newspaper into their boots and jackets for added insulation; they heated pebbles in cans over their campfires, then dumped the hot pebbles into their wet socks and the socks into their wet boots to try to dry them out. They also learned that if a man had been wounded, he had to keep moving or he would quickly freeze to death.

On January 8, Hitler authorized the withdrawal of his troops from the tip of the Bulge—a clear sign that he was at last giving up his offensive as a lost cause. German newspapers, which had headlined battle reports from the Ardennes since December 16, suddenly began featuring news from other fronts. And Hitler stopped giving top priority in supplies and replacement troops to the forces that a few weeks earlier had embodied his highest hopes.

By January 16, the two advancing American armies had linked up at Houffalize to clamp the pincers shut across the

On February 1, 1945, troops of the French First Army, hidden by a smoke screen, advance in the Colmar pocket, a German salient bulging 30 miles into the Alsace region. A French offensive in December had failed to reduce the salient significantly. But the second assault, launched on January 20 with the U.S. XXI Corps, cleared the pocket within three weeks.

Hitler's master plan for the Ardennes counteroffensive called for the Fifth and Sixth Panzer Armies to break through to Antwerp while the Seventh and Fifteenth Armies guarded their flanks. Had the Führer's plan succeeded, the Germans would have seized a vast chunk (red area) of Belgium and Luxembourg. But at their maximum penetration, the attackers managed only to bend the Allies' line back in a wedge-shaped bulge (gray-pink area) from which the battle got its name.

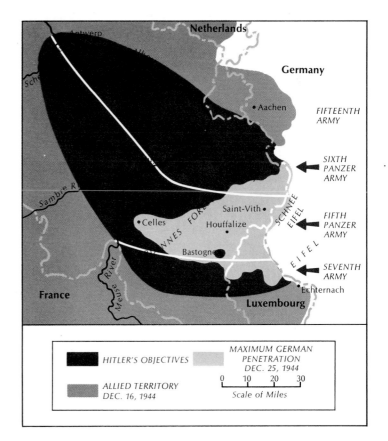

Bulge. There, they turned their attack eastward. Behind them came Graves Registration teams, searching for bodies in the snow and throwing them like sticks of frozen cordwood onto waiting trucks.

On Sunday, January 23, the 7th Armored Division attacked toward Saint-Vith. The honor of being the first unit to enter that ruined town fell to General Clarke's Combat Command B, the same outfit that had put up such a stubborn defense before being forced from the town exactly one month earlier.

By then, some of the Germans who had helped launch Hitler's offensive were already being withdrawn and sent off to other areas. The remnants of Dietrich's Sixth Panzer Army, leading the retreat, had been ordered to the Eastern Front to attempt to cut short the big Russian winter offensive that had broken out there on January 12. Others trudged back toward Germany in the bitter cold and snow, sick with dysentery, wounds, fatigue and defeat, their long, winding columns harried ceaselessly by pursuing tanks, artillery and fighter-bombers.

Many Germans never made it home. When the German losses were finally added up, the cost of Hitler's desperate gamble was about 100,000 casualties. The Americans also paid a stiff price: 80,987 casualties, including 10,276 killed, 47,493 wounded and 23,218 missing.

On January 28, 1945, the Battle of the Bulge was officially declared to be over. Although the German armies would then rally to defend their homeland, the last great assemblage of the Third Reich's precious reserves of men and matériel had been expended in the Ardennes. No doubt Eisenhower had been correct in guessing that the German offensive was an Allied opportunity and that it would shorten the war in Europe.

Even before the fighting in the Bulge ended, a bitter wrangle in the Allied high command threatened to blight the success of the hard-fought campaign. It began on December 29, when Field Marshal Montgomery sent a letter to General Eisenhower asking that he be elevated to the post of ground commander for all Allied forces in the west. He had held that post at the time of the Normandy invasion,

but had later relinquished it when all American units were placed under the command of General Bradley's Twelfth Army Group. Montgomery felt that, if only he had American forces again under his command, he would make short work of Germany.

To Eisenhower, Montgomery's letter seemed to reflect unfavorably on Bradley's ability—as well as on Eisenhower's judgment in trusting Bradley. Angrily, he drafted a cable to U.S. Army Chief of Staff General Marshall for the Combined Chiefs of Staff, saying that the time had finally arrived when they would have to choose between him and Montgomery.

But before the cable was sent, Eisenhower's chief of staff, Lieut. General Walter Bedell Smith, received a call from Montgomery's chief of staff, Major General Sir Francis de Guingand, who had got wind of the rift. They discussed its implications. There was no doubt that if the issue came to a head, Eisenhower—backed by overwhelming U.S. power—would win over Montgomery.

De Guingand prevailed on the Americans to delay the cable until he flew to Eisenhower's headquarters at Versailles and discussed the situation. There, he talked with Eisenhower and assured him that Montgomery had not realized the implications of his actions. He asked for time to reason with Montgomery.

Back in Brussels at Twenty-first Army Group headquarters, de Guingand told Montgomery that he was in serious danger of being fired, that the Americans felt so strongly about the matter that even Churchill would be powerless to prevent the change. De Guingand warned that the Americans liked Field Marshal Sir Harold Alexander, the Supreme Allied Commander in the Mediterranean, and would be happy to have him take Monty's place.

Montgomery reexamined his own position. Then he composed an apologetic letter to Ike, in which he said that he was "very distressed that my letter may have upset you and I would ask you to tear it up." Monty assured Eisenhower of his unqualified support.

Eisenhower was mollified and decided not to force the issue. But the whole ugly business flared up again when Montgomery held a press conference on January 7. Ironically, Montgomery had intended the conference as a conciliatory gesture to dispel the rancor between the British and American camps. Full of good will—and attired as usual in his casual combination of beret and jacket over wool sweater and corduroy slacks—Monty strode briskly into the hall to face the waiting reporters. He began explaining his own role in the action, but his words, to many ears, came out sounding wrong.

"As soon as I saw what was happening," Monty told the reporters, "I took certain steps to ensure that if the Germans got to the Meuse they would certainly not get over that river. And I carried out certain movements so as to provide balanced dispositions to meet the threatened danger. These were at the time merely precautions; i.e., I was thinking ahead." All this clearly suggested that Montgomery had masterminded the defense and saved the day. And though later he assured the reporters of his continued devotion to Ike and paid tribute to the American GI in the Bulge as a "first-class" soldier, the damage had been done.

The British press exacerbated the situation with stories alleging that Montgomery had foreseen the attack in the Ardennes and that he had pulled the American chestnuts out of the fire. At this point, with Bradley and his staff angry and dismayed, Montgomery was persuaded to write a pacifying letter to General Bradley, stating that it had been a great honor for him to have served with such fine American troops and commanders.

But it remained for Churchill to set the record straight. In a speech before the House of Commons on January 18, 1945, Churchill declared: "I have seen it suggested that the terrific battle which has been proceeding since December 16 on the American front is an Anglo-American battle. In fact, however, the United States troops have done almost all the fighting and have suffered almost all the losses. They have suffered losses almost equal to those on both sides in the battle of Gettysburg. I never hesitate to stand up for our own soldiers when their achievements have been cold-shouldered or neglected or overshadowed, as they sometimes are, but we must not forget that it is to American homes that the telegrams of personal losses and anxiety have been going during the past month. . . . Care must be taken not to claim for the British Army an undue share of what is undoubtedly the greatest American battle of the War, and will, I believe, be regarded as an ever-famous American victory."

Patrols of the American First and Third Armies meet near Houffalize, Belgium, on January 16, completing the pincer movement that cut off the Bulge at its waist. For both patrols, the trek to Houffalize had been an agonizing struggle against frigid weather and diehard German resistance. The First Army troops had spent nearly two weeks fighting 15 miles south from Grandménil and Manhay, and the GIs of the Third Army took a week to cover the seven miles from Bastogne. The bulk of the German forces were able to escape before the pincers snapped shut.

THE CIVILIANS' PLIGHT

Belgian civilians calmly await evacuation from La Gleize, the scene of Peiper's last stand. The townspeople endured days of shelling that routed the Germans.

HAPLESS FUGITIVES FROM THE FRONT

During a lull in the battle for an Ardennes town, a Belgian family crept out of their cellar refuge and found several wounded German soldiers lying on their floor. "They asked us," a family member recalled with heavy irony, " 'What are you doing here at the front?' "

As the citizens of the Ardennes quickly found out, the whole region was the front and there was no escaping it. For six weeks, the Battle of the Bulge swept back and forth over 2,000 square miles; some towns changed hands four times. The coming and going of armies was all too familiar: German forces had struck west through the region in 1914 and 1940, and the Allies had marched in to liberate the area just months earlier, in September 1944. Now the people of the Ardennes had the dubious distinction of being the only liberated Europeans to be reconquered by the Germans.

But the civilians would have fared much worse in the Battle of the Bulge had they not been veterans of war and experts at the art of survival. At the first sound of approaching gunfire, many of them quickly packed up bare necessities and set out for safety to the rear. Some spent days on the road, sleeping with relatives or friends, in churches or in refugee collection points, stretching the meager food given them by supply-short countrymen and U.S. troops. Those trapped by the German onslaught took to their cellars as the battle raged overhead. When the Americans recaptured a town, the citizens seized the chance to leave through friendly lines, fearing that the Germans might return.

By the time the bitter, seesaw struggle was finally over, more than 2,500 civilians had been killed. One man morbidly made a long list of the ways his friends and neighbors had perished: Miss Lennartz, in an air attack; Miss Solheid, of wounds suffered in Jacob Heindrich's house; Mrs. Hansen and a child, mortally hit while fleeing from one house to another; a woman from Engelsdorf, during an American attack that recaptured the town of Born. . . .

In a cold cellar in Marcourt, three women and a child try to sleep under a layer of blankets and a warm puppy. For as long as four weeks, the townspeople lived underground, rocked periodically by bombs exploding nearby. "We were rattled about like peas," recalled one woman.

A Belgian woman stoically appraises her ruined possessions in a stream of light pouring through a shell hole in the wall of her house near Lierneux. In the Ardennes towns and villages that were the hardest hit, only one house in 100 was left unscathed by the repeated and protracted shelling.

In recaptured Manhay, GIs cover an injured woman with blankets. Before the Germans were driven out, Manhay suffered raids by Allied fighter-bombers and 20

Volunteer cowhands of the U.S. 90th Division tend a herd whose owners had been sent to the rear.

minutes of shelling by eight U.S. artillery battalions.

A FRIENDLY EXCHANGE OF FOOD AND AID

The Battle of the Bulge produced an extraordinary cooperation between the U.S. Army and the Ardennes population. It was not just that the GIs and civilians faced a common enemy; their solidarity was born of a genuine friendship for each other.

The Americans did all they could to relieve the Belgians' plight in the terrible battle. The soldiers, sometimes short of food themselves, shared their rations with civilian refugees and set up soup kitchens at evacuation centers in the rear. They tended evacuees' livestock. They helped dig out wounded Belgians trapped in their shell-battered homes.

They soon came to realize that the Belgians were doing much more for them.

In German-held areas, townspeople risked their lives by sheltering lost or wounded GIs. Civilians misdirected German tank columns, winning precious time for the Americans to regroup in the confusion. In the besieged town of Bastogne, citizens emptied their own pharmacies of medicines the Americans lacked.

Behind the shifting lines, in towns held by American troops and already crowded with refugees, civilian authorities invited the soldiers to occupy any public buildings they needed. Private citizens billeted and fed Americans. Belgians resoled GI boots, repaired truck tires and dug trenches to free soldiers for combat.

Housewives helped with a unique, poignant sacrifice. They came forward with their linens—many of them priceless heirlooms—for the Americans to use as winter camouflage *(overleaf)*.

Bed sheets and lace-trimmed tablecloths, donated for winter camouflage by Belgian women, are used to cover a variety of American vehicles and a gun.

RETURNING HOME AND BEGINNING AGAIN

Those civilians who had left their towns and villages in advance of the German onslaught returned home as soon as the resurgent American forces had driven the Germans a safe distance away. Many Belgians found that home was now a shell-blasted house, in need of extensive repair or complete rebuilding.

Much of the damage had been done by Americans, and some of it could have been avoided. The destruction of Malmédy by no less than three errant American bombing raids prompted some GIs to call their own airmen the "American Luftwaffe." But the civilians almost never lodged any protests. "We can stand the bombs," one Belgian patriot explained. "That's nothing. But the Germans—we couldn't stand the Germans here again."

Swathed in a neatly wrapped bedroll, a refugee heads homeward with his dog as Army trucks roll by.

Civilians survey the smoking ruins of Malmédy. One eyewitness said that the thrice-bombed town was "reduced to a burned-out pile of cinders and rubble."

A refugee and his wife stand in front of their demolished house while she weeps bitterly, shielding her eyes from the awful sight of the wreckage and loss.

Camping on the street, members of a Belgian family prepare to rebuild their wrecked home in heavily bombed Houffalize.

Belgian boys shovel debris off their front steps in Lierneux, the scene of fierce house-to-house fighting around Christmas.

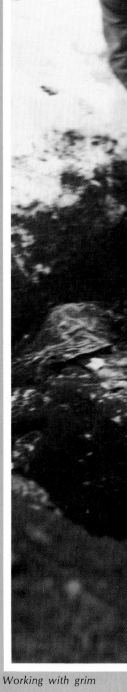

Working with grim

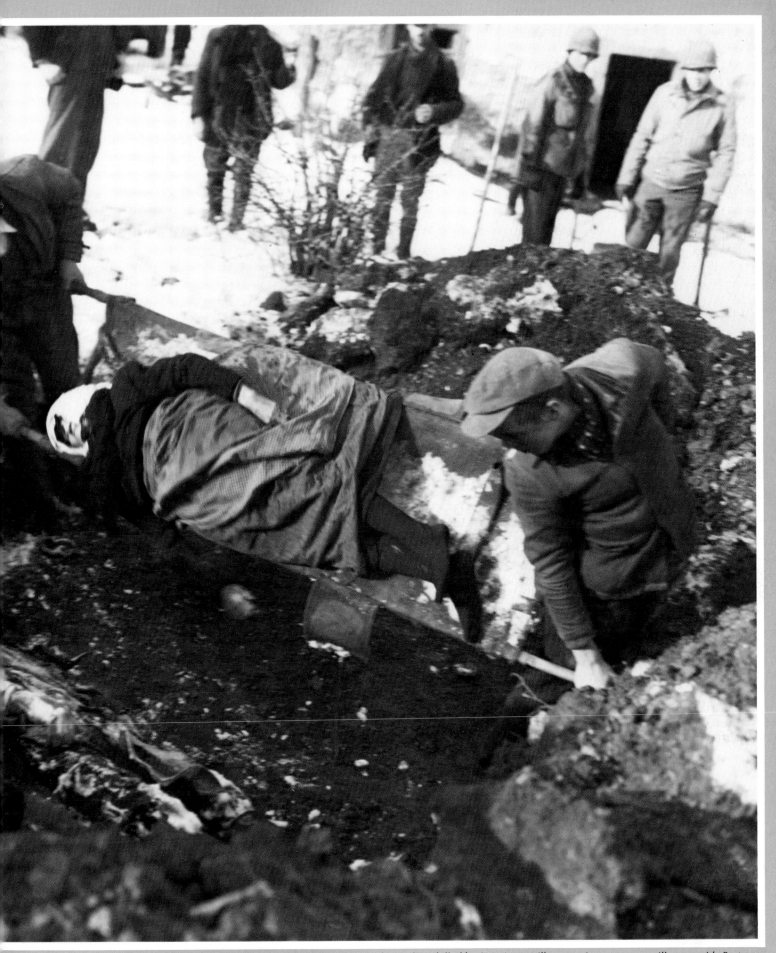

efficiency, two Belgians roll the corpse of a woman into a common grave for civilians killed by American artillery near Lutremange, a village outside Bastogne.

Jerome Ballen (left), a Belgian policeman who served as an infantryman with the U.S. 1st Division through the Battle of the Bulge, fought on into Germany beside his GI friend Sergeant Hugh Coltran. Ballen's buddies called him "Sergeant" and passed the hat to raise a sergeant's pay for him.

AN OLD ALLY REJOINS THE WAR

The Belgians' yeoman efforts to help the cause of their liberators did not stop with the Battle of the Bulge.

After the Ardennes had once again been cleared of Germans, a number of Belgian military units served with the Allied forces for the rest of the War. Belgian railroad crews repaired tracks and worked aboard the trains that sped cargoes from Antwerp and Ostend to the advancing front. Belgian coal miners worked overtime to fuel the trains and the reopened factories. By April of 1945, the Belgians were manufacturing an assortment of war goods: ammunition, uniforms, bridge girders, mess equipment and tank treads.

In helping the Allies, the Belgian people helped themselves: The booming industries put the long-suffering nation well on the road to economic recovery before the end of the War.

As proud Belgian miners look on, their grinning representative presents an